Mentor for Life

Mentor for Life

Leader's Training Manual

Equipping Small Group Leaders
to Intentionally Make Disciples

Natasha Sistrunk Robinson

credo
house publishers

Mentor for Life Training Resource Guide

Copyright © 2017 by Natasha Sistrunk Robinson

Published in the United States by Credo House Publishers,
a division of Credo Communications, LLC, Grand Rapids, Michigan
www.credohousepublishers.com

Requests for information or inquires about reproducing material from this work should be addressed to Natasha Sistrunk Robinson through her website, www.natashaSrobinson.com.

Natasha Sistrunk Robinson is the Visionary Founder of Leadership LINKS, Inc. The organization offers leadership education that facilitates impactful living, character and spiritual development. Offering this resource directly supports the organization's mission. To find out more about Leadership LINKS, Inc., visit their website, www.leadershiplinksus.org.

ISBN: 978-1-625860-78-1

Art direction: Holly Sharp Creative
Interior design: Kirstin Hunt

Printed in the United States of America

Second edition

To all my mentors, near and far, here and gone. You know who you are.

Thank you.

About the Author

Natasha Sistrunk Robinson is the author of *Mentor for Life: Finding Purpose through Intentional Discipleship*. She intentionally serves as a credible witness of Christ's leadership to engage, equip, and empower people to live and lead on purpose. She is the visionary founder of Leadership LINKS, Inc., a Bible teacher, freelance writer, anti-human trafficking advocate, and champion for education. Natasha is a graduate of Gordon-Conwell Theological Seminary Charlotte (*cum laude*, M.A. Christian Leadership) and the U.S. Naval Academy. A former Marine Corps officer, she has over fifteen years of leadership and mentoring experience in the military, government, church, seminary, and non-profit sectors. She is a sought after leadership consultant, mentoring coach, and speaker. Connect via her official website www.NatashaSRobinson.com, blog www.asistasjourney.com, Twitter @asistasjourney, or www.facebook.com/NatashaSistrunkRobinson.

Acknowledgments

My sincere thanks and appreciation for all the women of the Women's Mentoring Ministry in Greensboro, North Carolina including: my ministry partner, Nikki Kober, and team, Melva Walker, Susan Blankenship, Selma Rummage, Debbie Hahn, Mary Kober, Nany Byrd, Carmen Lowery, Lynn Graham, Lea Joyce, Judy Averitte, Charlotte Perkins, Jennifer Byrd, Katie Long, Roena Stallsmith and Joy Peterson. You have influenced, shaped, and lived this resource. Special thanks to the editors of *Christianity Today*, and to the faculty of Gordon-Conwell Theological Seminary Charlotte.

A Word of Welcome

Welcome to the *Mentor for Life* Leadership Training Resource. This resource provides training for practical application of the mentoring vision and commitments shared in the book, *Mentor for Life: Finding Purpose Through Intentional Discipleship*. It would be most beneficial to read that book prior to or in conjunction with completing this training with your leadership team.

This resource is separated into two sections:

Part I includes three short essays. The first essay, *Identifying and Training Leaders*, is for you as you prayerfully consider the right people to invite for service on the mentoring leadership team. Mentors on the leadership team can also use this essay as a guide when prayerfully seeking to identify mentees within their group who have potential to become future mentors or join the mentoring leadership team. The second essay, *Christian Leader as Mentor*, will help potential mentors understand their responsibilities as Christian leaders. This essay will be beneficial group discussion for the entire mentoring leadership team. The third essay, *What to Expect from Your Mentoring Relationship*, is critical for establishing the foundation and expectations of the mentoring relationships. I recommend mentors review this essay with their mentees at the forming of their mentoring relationships. These guidelines can help them establish terms of agreement, mutual commitments, and ensure a safe mentoring community.

Part II is a six lesson leadership training curriculum for mentoring ministry leaders and their leadership teams. This section includes the bare essentials for understanding and equipping yourself and others to mentor well. Much of the information shared is also valuable content, training, and reference for those who simply want to start a mentoring group in their home.

Ministry leaders' take notice that there are additional preparation notes for you at the end of this resource. I recommend that you review the first couple preparation notes before you start training with your leadership team, and the remaining notes as preparation for the accompanying lessons. Also pay special attention to Appendix B: "Getting Started: Mentoring Ministry Checklist." These notes will equip you to prepare for leadership training, build the mentoring leadership team, and set the tone and expectations for a loving and nurturing learning experience.

The fact that you hold this resource in your hand tells me that you are bold and courageous to carefully consider the Lord's command to make disciples. I am excited about what the Lord will do through your faithful obedience to this call! Christ himself goes before you. Mentoring for God's purposes is an act of obedience. Pray often. I trust that this resource will assist in your efforts to prepare and plan effectively. I am here to help you along the way, and pray this experience will be transformative for you, in addition to blessing your church, ministry, and others in your areas of influence for many years to come. You can share your learning and encourage others to faithfully pursue the mentoring mission by using the hashtag #Mentor4Life.

For His Glory,

Natasha Sistrunk Robinson

Contents

Essay One

Identifying and Training Mentor Leaders

Jesus selected the twelve disciples after spending an entire night in prayer.[1] There was no recruiting, applications, letters of recommendation, or referrals. He certainly did not take "volunteers." Jesus simply prayed, selected the disciples his Father revealed, and gave them a choice to participate in his missional task. When we *Mentor for Life*, we use this simple yet biblical practice as a guide when inviting others to mentor, shepherd, and care for fragile souls. Mentoring requires a serious commitment of humble, servant leaders who are willing to consistently sacrifice, passionately pursue Christ, and faithfully consider the needs of others above themselves.[2] If a prospective mentor is not fully committed to the work, he or she should not do it. Therefore, praying for God's direction concerning potential mentor leaders is a radical first step for developing a mentoring leadership team.

Upon careful observation, the church is one of very few organizations where people are allowed to volunteer and then be placed in lay leadership positions with no serious evaluation or training. This practice is irresponsible and it must stop! In the church, we are God's agents for winning souls and shepherding them. This work is more important than anything that takes place in the "secular" work arena and requires more caution and care. Therefore, we prayerfully seek the Lord to confirm mentor leaders, and we commit to their continuous education and training so they are equipped for this work of service.[3]

What do we look for in a potential mentor leader? There are two lenses in which to prayerfully consider potential mentors: character and commitment. As a faithful mentor to his disciple Timothy, the Apostle Paul gave him clear guidelines: "set an example for believers in speech, in life, in love, in faith, and in purity…devote yourself to the public reading of Scripture, to preaching and to teaching. Do not neglect your gift…be diligent in these matters; give yourself wholly to them, so that everyone may see your progress" (1 Tim. 4: 11-15)." In these verses, Paul summarizes the importance of character and commitment. He assumes that people will evaluate Timothy by observing the faithfulness of his life. The way Timothy commits to his relationships, studies and shares the Word of God, and diligently exercises his spiritual gifts must be shining examples of his personal relationship with Christ, giving him a good reputation among his fellow servants and casual observers. A person who mentors as intentional discipleship must also have a good reputation in the church and in the world.[4] This does not mean that a potential mentor must be perfect or have a spotless past. Only Jesus would meet those qualifications. On the other hand, it does mean that a potential mentor must wholeheartedly seek the Lord, persevere in the faith, and have a humble and healthy posture of confession and repentance when they do fall.

Paul's teaching on this matter of character and leadership expands throughout 1 Timothy chapters three and four. He concludes with the most important instruction that Timothy and those he teaches must "train themselves to be godly" (1 Tim. 4: 7b). The godly characteristics we look for in potential mentors are: humility, teachable spirit, servant's heart, commitment, and spiritual maturity.[5] With these considerations, prayerfully contemplate the people God reveals as potential mentors for the leadership team. Then ask those people to prayerfully consider participating in your mentoring training program. Explain the expectations for the training program and the commitment it entails so they are able to make an informed decision.[6]

During leadership training, your responsibility is to equip potential mentors for this important work of accepting God's mentoring mission. According to Peter Drucker's interview of Father Leo Bartel, "if people are properly motivated…developing competence becomes part of their very need. My biggest difficulty in asking people to serve is that they are painfully aware of their lack of experience and lack of preparation. If we can provide them with that, they're eager to learn."[7] With the *Mentor for Life* book and this training resource, you can give potential mentors the preparation which builds their confidence to lead well and know they are not alone in this process. God is with them. You are with them, and they will have a team who regularly encourages and supports them throughout the mentoring season as they continue to receive ongoing training and encouragement.

During training, it is incumbent that you share the conviction that Christian leaders accept the responsibility to mentor as intentional discipleship because it pleases God. Mentoring glorifies God, shares the gospel's message, advances God's kingdom agenda, causes disciples to live their lives on purpose, teaches disciples to love and be loved well, and encourages them to do good works. Mentoring also provides an opportunity to develop friendships within our spiritual family and nurtures a safe community, with a commitment to openness, oneness, authenticity, grace, love, and multiplication. Jesus taught his disciples with this understanding. From his teaching in John 15:12-15, it is clear that in his training grounds, the disciples become friends who focused on their master's mission together. Likewise, offering an effective and high quality mentoring training program enables you to evaluate the potential mentor's level of commitment, provide teaching and growing opportunities for them, and give them the opportunity to make an informed decision before starting their own mentoring group. They should make that decision upon the completion of their mentoring leadership training.

Do not regard potential mentors as volunteers. Contrary to popular opinion, they are not! The church is not an all-volunteer work force. The church is a mighty work force empowered by the Holy Spirit, and when given godly perspective and proper training, we have the ability to do together what seems impossible. Relate to all potential mentors as faithful servants (which sometimes feels like non-paid workers) who are on a critical life mission for the tasks God has placed before the collective "you." As a ministry leader, you cannot faithfully accomplish the work of the ministry without the mentors and therefore, I encourage you to hold them in high regard and to high standards. Concerning volunteers and unpaid staff, I agree with Father Leo Bartel, former Vicar of Social Ministry of the Catholic Diocese of Rockford, Illinois:

> Have high expectations for them [lay leadership]. I believe firmly that people will tend to live up to the expectations that others have for them. And I try, as best I can, to hold high expectations for the people around me, and in many cases they seem to find this a compliment. They seem to be honored that I would expect them to do well. And they come back looking for ways to improve, eager for opportunities to become more and more competent.[8]

Often times, the lack of confidence—not competence—is the greatest leadership crisis. As the leader, you address this challenge by offering biblical perspective and solid training to equip potential mentors to serve well.

This work of mentoring as intentional discipleship is more important than anything they may be called to do because it consistently sets godly priorities before them which has eternal implications. Individually and collectively as a local church, we cannot effectively do everything well but "there is no greater achievement than to help a few people get the right things done. That's perhaps the only satisfactory definition of being a leader."[9] This is your challenge for leading and mentoring: *As disciples of Christ, consistently put the challenge before mentors to get the right things done and encourage them to do the same for those they are called to disciple.*

Having the Initial Conversations with Potential Mentor Leaders

As I have mentored, trained, and coached others, people often ask, "What characteristics do you look for when considering who can effectively lead mentoring small groups?" I recommend that you start by asking yourself and others in your ministry context basic questions like:

How do you know if you or someone else is a good person to mentor others?

What fears would keep you from mentoring others?

What are the qualifications or characteristics of a godly mentor, particularly when considering your ministry context, potential mentoring ministry team, and identified communal needs?

Characteristics of a Godly Mentor:

1. Humility – A humble person is self-aware, for "humility is honestly assessing ourselves in light of God's holiness and our sinfulness…All genuine humility is rooted in: God's holiness and our sinfulness."[10] A humble mentor does not seek to impose her will onto the life of another or to elevate herself above her sister. Rather, a humble mentor generously offers herself to her mentees. She is other-centered. She thinks of God first and then of those she is called to mentor.

Meditate on God's Word:

This is the one I esteem: he who is humble and contrite in spirit, and trembles at my word (Isa. 66:2b).

Do nothing out of selfish ambition or vain conceit, but in humility consider others better than yourselves. Each of you should look not only to your own interests, but also to the interests of others (Phil. 2:3-4).

2. Teachable Spirit – An excellent mentor understands that she does not know it all and has therefore submitted herself to the mentorship or leadership of another. She is willing to become a life-long learner. She is a student of the Bible, a student of her own community, and a student of those she is called to serve. An emerging leader sometimes struggles with followership or authority issues. Often times we lead well first by learning to follow, so emerging leaders must learn obedience through submission—first to God and then to God's appointed leaders.[11]

Meditate on God's Word:

Submit yourself for the Lord's sake to every authority instituted among men: whether to the king, as the supreme authority, or to governors, who are sent by him to punish those who do wrong and to commend those who do right (1 Peter 2:13-14).

Now the Bereans were of more noble character than the Thessalonians, for they received the message with great eagerness and examined the Scriptures every day to see if what Paul said was true (Acts 17:11).

3. Servant's Heart – A mentor is a leader which means she is responsible for serving the people God has graciously allowed her to influence. A godly mentor sacrifices for the sake of the other.

Meditate on God's Word:

Jesus called them together and said, "You know that the rulers of the Gentiles lord it over them, and their high officials exercise authority over them. Not so with you. Instead, whoever wants to become great among you must be your servant, and whoever wants to be first must be your slave—just as the Son of Man did not come to be served, but to serve, and to give his life as a ransom for many (Matt. 20:25-28).

Serve wholeheartedly, as if you were serving the Lord, not men, because you know that the Lord will reward everyone for whatever good he does, whether he is slave or free (Eph. 6:7-8).

4. Commitment – Discipleship is a long-term commitment. Jesus journeyed with his disciples for approximately three years. If we expect to truly disciple someone for God's kingdom purposes, we must commit to consistently invest time. Discipleship is time consuming and can be quite frustrating, especially when mentees continue to make mistakes, you do not see the desired transformation within "your" expected time frame, or you begin to question whether your investment matters at all. In those challenging moments, it is important to remember that God is with you, God has an end in mind, and He alone is responsible for transforming hearts and causing all of our lives to bear fruit. Ask God for his help to sustain your mentoring journey.

Meditate on God's Word:

Let us not become weary in doing good, for at the proper time we will reap a harvest if we do not give up. Therefore, as we have opportunity, let us do good to all people especially to those who belong to the family of believers (Gal. 6:9-10).

Never be lacking in zeal, but keep your spiritual fervor, serving the Lord (Rom. 12:11).

5. Maturity – A potential mentor must be emotionally and spiritually healthy. This means that an effective mentor is not someone who harbors unforgiveness or bitterness in her heart from unresolved life issues. Hurt people hurt other people. It is quite possible for someone to have a sincere desire to mentor, but not have the emotional capacity, maturity, or healing necessary to mentor effectively at a particular time. As a ministry leader, you do not want mentors ministering their personal hurts or projecting their own pain, losses, or unresolved issues onto others. Also, a spiritually mature person will live with integrity and have a good reputation among others.

The Word of God for You:

Whatever happens, conduct yourselves in a manner worthy of the gospel of Christ (Phil. 1:27).

Live such good lives among the pagans that, though they accuse you of doing wrong, they may see your good deeds and glorify God on the day he visits us (1 Peter 2:12).

Replacing a Volunteer Attitude with a Call to the Mentoring Mission:

A commitment to mentoring for God's kingdom purposes is counter-culture to the world and in the modern American church. In most churches, leaders see a need or begin a new church ministry, and they ask for volunteers to serve in that ministry. If this is the natural inclination of your church, let me say plainly that you do not want volunteers to mentor. The idea of selecting mentors may be foreign and unpopular to us, but it is indeed a practice we observe in the scriptures. What lessons can we glean from Jesus' selection of his twelve disciples?

- Pray: Jesus selected the disciples after spending an entire night in prayer (Luke 6:12-13).

- Make Selections & Ask for the Commitment: The problem with volunteers is that they normally agree because they like the idea of what you have asked them to do, but once they get into actually doing the hard work, their passion and commitment can waiver. When Jesus prayerfully selected his disciples, he gave them the choice as to whether or not they would follow him. They would be required to give up everything (Luke 14:26-27) and yield to the work of their Savior. True disciples of Christ commit to make disciples because of who Christ is, and what He has already done in their lives.

- Train Mentors to do the Work: After Jesus compelled his disciples to follow him, he began a training program which prepared them to minister and make disciples of others long after he was physically gone from their presence. The church is one of very few organizations where people are allowed to volunteer and then be placed "in charge" with no real evaluation or training. A salaried job will sometimes require employees to go through a three month evaluation and training period before receiving all their benefits and their security as a full-time employee. The work of caring for souls is much more important than any work that takes place in a "secular" work environment, and must therefore be approached with much more responsibility and care. Providing quality leadership training for potential mentors has three benefits:

  1. Develop Confidence: I have heard it said, "You do not have to know everything or have all of the answers when mentoring, you just need to be one step ahead of those you have been called to mentor." It is quite natural for people to become nervous that they will be exposed for their lack of knowledge or incompetence. As leaders, we have a responsibility "to prepare God's people for works of service, so that the body of Christ may be built up until we all reach unity in the faith and in the knowledge of the Son of God and become

mature (Eph. 4:12–13a).[12] The *Mentor for Life* book, this resource, and accompanying videos will assist you in this effort.

2. Set High Expectations Upfront: Do not forget the words of Father Leo Bartel, and encourage mentors to set standards for providing a safe, intimate, and mutually beneficial learning community within their mentoring groups.

3. Remember: *Mentoring as intentional discipleship* is important and necessary kingdom work. Make sure mentors understand and never forget this. Stay focused. Be encouraging. Celebrate small wins. Together, find joy on the mentoring journey.

Leading and Equipping Mentors:

- Lead by example: Being one step ahead means that you do not ask mentor leaders to do anything you have not already done, and that mentors do not ask mentees to do anything they have not already done. Take the first steps and lead with integrity.

- Equip: Preparing mentors for works of service so the body of Christ can grow in maturity, be united in faith, and in knowledge of Christ (Eph. 4:11–16). The leadership team is where mentors can practice the spiritual disciplines and experience accountability, while nurturing a safe community and healthy relationships.

- Team Building: Training mentors together builds camaraderie; creates a thinking, serving, and mutually edifying support group, and allows for an endless amount of resources and experiences amongst the ministry leadership team.

- Soul Care: Meeting or identifying the spiritual and emotional needs of the mentor so that she can love and serve others well.

Essay Two

Christian Leader as Mentor

In the midst of conversations about ministry needs, work obligations, and church growth, Christian leaders sometimes lose focus of the priority to intentionally make disciples. People and the loving care of their souls is the ministry work of all followers of Christ and we must not lose sight of it. Mentoring for God's purposes reminds us to make people our priority.

Mentoring is a trusted partnership where people share wisdom that fosters spiritual growth and leads to transformation as mentors and mentees[13] grow in their love of Christ, knowledge of self, and love of others.

Defining mentoring in these terms affirms that mentoring is the responsibility of all Christians, and our primary Christian calling is to make disciples of Jesus Christ. Although we may receive different spiritual assignments—both formal and informal—along our Christian journey, the call to mentoring is universal. We are all called to mentoring relationships where disciples are encouraged to *know and love God, know who they are in Christ Jesus, and love their neighbors.* Accepting this responsibility requires our understanding and ownership of the definition of mentoring as presented. After a brief explanation of this mentoring definition, this short essay answers the question, "Why mentor?" and presents a relational and communal focus of mentoring through the teaching and life of Jesus.

While Merriam-Webster defines mentor as a trusted counselor, guide, tutor, or coach,[14] mentoring from the perspective of intentional discipleship means that God's kingdom purposes for mentorship and discipleship are one and the same. The words can be used synonymously only when a Christian assumes the responsibility of influence in the life of another for the purpose of drawing the mentee into an intimate relationship of following Christ. God uses mentoring to sanctify individuals and transform them into the image of Jesus Christ (Rom. 8:29). We make mentoring our priority because Jesus made discipleship his priority (Matt. 28:19-20). By neglecting the responsibility of mentoring, we are doing a disservice to those we are called to serve. Understanding this responsibility, however, can have a tremendous impact on the Church.

The good news is that God has not left us alone on this faith journey. The Holy Spirit empowers us to accept the responsibility to mentor in a sacrificial act that glorifies God. When we mentor, we share the message of the whole gospel, advance God's kingdom mission, challenge disciples to live their lives on purpose, teach them to love well, and equip them for works of righteousness. Mentoring is mutually beneficial and has the same transformative effects on the mentor and mentee. Mentoring in this way is simply an act of obedience.

While the Bible does present several key one-on-one mentoring relationships—or what I would refer to as divine appointments—those relationships were uniquely orchestrated by God for a specific purpose at a specific time.[15] God still does the divine work of assigning one mentor to a particular person for His own purposes, although those one-on-one relationships are generally not arranged by a third party. Therefore, the *Mentor for Life* model is communal through the small group or mentoring community of no more than six mentees. When we mentor for life, we follow the relational model of Jesus and his twelve apostles. Jesus invested his time in mentoring a small group of people so they could partake in God's redemptive story, make disciples of Jesus, and understand their calling and purpose to live on mission for God.

Mentoring is foundational to God's redemptive story because it fulfills the cultural mandate of Genesis 1:28 and the great commission of Matthew 28:19-20. In the beginning of his good creation, God said, "It is not good for man to be alone" (Genesis 2:18a [NIV]). Therefore, mentoring provides an opportunity for companionship with an open embrace of vulnerability and love. Jesus mentored his disciples with this understanding when he stated in John 15:12-15:

> My commandment is this: Love each other as I have loved you. Greater love has no one than this, that he lay down his life for his friends. You are my friends if you do what I command. I no longer call you servants, because a servant does not know his master's business. Instead, I have called you friends, for everything that I learned from my Father I have made known to you.

Mentoring brings the master's business into focus. The master's kingdom mission is to build a family of worshippers for himself; for in the end and with his life, Christ has purchased people from every tribe, nation, and language to worship him (Rev. 5:9-12 and 7:4-10). When Christian leaders make the commitment to mentor and make disciples of all nations, they are embracing the whole gospel and essentially saying to God, "your kingdom come, your will be done on earth as it is in heaven" (Matt. 6:10). Like Jesus, Christian leaders are able to mentor effectively by putting all personal relationships into proper perspective.

Throughout his life, Jesus revealed that the gospel is not simply shared. It is also lived through communal relationships. Concerning the greatest commandment, Jesus stated, "Love the Lord your God with all your heart and with all your soul and with all your mind and with all your strength…Love your neighbor as yourself" (Mark 12:30-31a). A healthy mentoring relationship first encourages a disciple to *know and love God*. Secondly, it helps the disciple *understand his or her identity in Christ Jesus*. Finally, it encourages disciples to *love their neighbors*.

Mentoring through Relationships

Assuming a mentoring relationship is a sacred and sacrificial responsibility, it must be approached humbly with the full understanding that the Holy Spirit works to change the hearts of humans.[16] Christian leaders must not attempt to take on that divine responsibility, but rather surrender total transformation to God. Dr. Rick D. Moore writes, "The goal of mentoring…is 'a difficult thing…indeed it involves an element of the spirit that cannot be packaged, manipulated or controlled."[17] While the Holy Spirit works to change hearts, the human agency of mentoring can facilitate the process of renewing a disciple's mind. The heart and mind are intimately connected; both reveal our love, longing, and the true nature of our will. As a mentor, Christian leaders teach disciples to put off their old self and become new in the attitude of their minds by imitating God and walking in true righteousness and holiness (Eph. 4:22-24).

Through mentoring, Christian leaders accept the responsibility to teach and train disciples to live worthy of the calling they have received in Christ Jesus (Eph. 4:1). This teaching is beneficial to the individual, the Christian family, and the world at large. This theology has practical application because mentoring well includes considerations for how we think and how we act as ambassadors of Christ on this earth. Mentoring encourages disciples to open their eyes, see the needs of the world, and put their faith into action by responding with compassion and justice towards others.[18] Mentoring renews the minds of disciples by reflecting on the habits of the intentional thought and conversation, and by developing a contemplative mind.[19] Therefore, mentoring helps a disciple make wise choices by cultivating their theology and Christian worldview. This growth first begins with a disciple's relationship with God.

Mentors encourage disciples to constantly renew their relationship with God. A.W. Tozer writes, "What comes to our minds when we think about God is the most important thing about us."[20] What you think about God shapes your whole attitude towards him. Unfortunately, many disciples struggle on their Christian journey because they have an inaccurate view of God. Mentors encourage disciples to go to God's inerrant Word to discover the Triune God for themselves. Disciples need to know the one, true God who is *both* merciful, gracious, loving *and* holy, just, and righteous. This is the God Christians are called to sacrificially emulate.

The Apostle Paul wrote to the church of Ephesus, "Be imitators of God, therefore, as dearly loved children and live a life of love, just as Christ loved us and gave himself up for us as a fragrant offering and sacrifice to God" (Eph. 5:1-2). Again, Christ is presented as an example of how Christians live. As disciples grow in their love and knowledge of God, they also grow in their identity and find their purpose in Christ Jesus. Robert J. Wicks writes, "Perhaps the most critical koan [puzzle] we face in life is, 'Who am I really?' Through the mentoring relationship, we explore ways to gain sufficient freedom and inner ease to be who we really are so that we, in turn, can be a helping presence to others."[21] In the post-modern society where technology constantly sends false messages, disciples must hold fast to God's truth, finding their identity and purpose in Christ alone. This valuable understanding builds confidence and sets a clear direction for work[22] and building healthy relationships. When disciples know and love God and know who they are in Christ Jesus, they can also grow to love their neighbors well.

In the parable of the good Samaritan, Jesus again offered teaching about the love for one's neighbor (Luke 10:25-37). He closed the parable lesson by telling the disciples to go and live like the Samaritan. Jesus practiced what he preached and literally laid down his life for the sake of his neighbors and friends. In the same manner, he says, disciples are his friends only *if* they sacrificially lay down their lives for the sake of others (John 15:13-14).

In conclusion, all Christian are called to mentor, follow Christ's example, and encourage other disciples to live sacrificially for the sake of the gospel. Of her passion for mentoring, Darlene Zschech wrote, "it is my deepest desire to remind leaders everywhere that the kingdom of God is about people and that we are not here to build our own kingdoms but to bring God's kingdom into the lives of others. A life lived in Christ is a sacrificial life—a life poured out, a life lived to lift the lives of others."[23] Christians everywhere are called to make God's will and name known on earth by establishing mentoring relationships where disciples are encouraged *to know and love God, know who they are in Christ Jesus, and love their neighbors*. We commit to the work of mentoring so all disciples can love well, live lives on purpose, commit to God's holy work, and model the example of Jesus Christ.

Essay Three

What to Expect from Your Mentoring Relationship

When Jesus called his disciples to follow him, they left their jobs, homes, work, and communities to obey his calling. They left the familiar in order to travel unknown territory because they believed He was the Messiah (or "Anointed One" of God). As disciples of Christ, Jesus calls us to an obedient response to follow him and to make disciples of others. Being a disciple of Christ means that we lay aside our old life, and embrace the new life that is pleasing to God. The good news is that God himself promises to change us and be with us on our spiritual journey. He promises never to leave us or forsake us. He has also adopted us into his new family. This family, called "the church" or community of believers, are the people of God who commit to grow, serve, fellowship (spending intentional and quality time together), pray, and worship God together. We know that we are in desperate need of God, and trust that he has graciously offered us his presence and support through human relationships. Growing together as an intimate family of believers is what you can expect from your mentoring experience.

In Luke 14:25-35, Jesus teaches that followers must consider the cost of discipleship. He also states, "Any of you who does not give up everything he has cannot be my disciple" (v. 33). Do you think this sounds like a tough, if not impossible order? You are correct! Jesus is not asking you to do anything in your own power or in your own strength. On the other hand, he is being very clear that He wants first place in your life. According to the Bible, being a disciple of Christ is not about saying a prayer, being a "do-gooder" or faithful church goer, and it is not even about our religious practices. Being a disciple of Christ reflects our willingness to submit our lives to his authority and to embrace his kingdom mission and purpose for us.

When we commit to follow Jesus, the Bible says that we receive God's supernatural help through the power of the Holy Spirit. He has also placed others in our lives to help us along the way. From the beginning, God has stated, "It is not good for the man to be alone" (Gen. 2:18). Therefore, our help also comes from joining in community with other believers. You can grow in your faith and receive God's help through a mentoring community.

Mentoring is a trusted partnership through which one or several persons share wisdom which fosters spiritual growth and leads to transformed lives of both mentor and mentee(s), as each grows in their love of Jesus Christ, knowledge of self, and love of their neighbors.

Mentoring is a mutual commitment. Your mentor will commit to serving you on your faith journey. Actually, you can expect accountability from your mentor and others in your mentoring group. At the beginning of the mentoring season, you will be asked to sign a covenant or agree to a mentoring group affirmation. Remember, we must all consider the cost of discipleship.[24] God is faithful to keep his promises to us, and one way you can model God's character is by keeping the commitment you make to your mentoring community. After all, the writer of Ecclesiastes wrote, "It is better not to vow than to make a vow and not fulfill it" (Ecc. 5:5). Consider carefully before you commit to a mentoring relationship.

In a mentoring group, you must agree to maintain a safe community. This means that you commit to trust others with all of you, and you also agree to present yourself trustworthy to the other people in your group. You agree to being a safe person who is helpful, a present listener, a truth speaker, and an avid encourager. You commit to learning to love others well, making peace and not harming others with your words. Through mentoring, you covenant not to let "unwholesome talk come out of your mouth, but only what is helpful for building others up *according to their needs*, that it may benefit those who listen" (Eph. 4:29, emphasis added).

The same six mentoring commitments presented in *Mentor for Life* are asked of you, your mentor, and your mentoring peers. These commitments include: 1.) presence, 2.) discipline, 3.) mission, 4.) community, 5.) relationships, and 6.) love.

- Presence: Being present with God and present in community with other disciples is essential for our spiritual transformation.

- Discipline: Cultivating spiritual disciplines help us recognize our spiritual poverty and desperate need for God.

- Mission: Understanding God's kingdom mission gives us an urgency and intentionality to run our own spiritual race and to invite others to win on the journey of following Christ.

- Community: Committing to safe and trusting mentoring relationships provides encouragement, accountability, and support.

- Relationships: Mentoring requires that we embrace people as God does and welcome diverse relationships that reflect true unity in the Body of Christ.

- Love: Mentoring is a continuous sacrificial and selfless act of love which shapes our character, clarifies our spiritual gifts, and affirms our purpose and calling.

Understanding and embracing these commitments will help you grow and thrive on your mentoring and faith journey. These mentoring commitments will also ensure a safe, loving, and learning mentoring community. By taking ownership of these commitments, you and your mentoring peers will know what to expect from your mentoring relationships.

Lesson One:

Mentor for Freedom

Building a Foundation of Mentoring: It's Relational

Preparation for Lesson I

PERSONAL EXERCISE FOR THE LESSON: Exercise instructions included on next page – Bring a short biography or your life story, and your faith testimony to share with the group. Your biography should be one paragraph, and your testimony should be no longer than one page.

Required Reading (Note: This material must be read prior to the team's lesson):

- *Mentor for Life: Finding Purpose Through Intentional Discipleship*, Chapters 1–3
- "Christian Leader as Mentor" Essay (provided in Part I of this resource)
- Mentoring Resource Reading: Optional

DEFINITION OF MENTORING

Mentoring is a trusted partnership where people share wisdom that fosters spiritual growth and leads to transformation, as mentors and mentees grow in their love of Christ, knowledge of self, and love of others.

PURPOSE OF THIS LESSON:

Develop relationships among leaders in the training program, get a general overview of the mentoring principles, and encourage all to take the risk of mentoring. Begin to collaboratively develop a vision that allows you to apply the mentoring principles to your own ministry context.

OBJECTIVE

The prospective mentor will develop and embrace a foundational understanding of mentoring as intentional discipleship for God's kingdom purposes.

GOALS

1) The prospective mentor will share a personal testimony about his or her relationship with God.

2.) The prospective mentor will effectively communicate the mission of mentoring for the purpose of drawing others into proper relationship with God and into Christian community.

"HOW TO SHARE A PERSONAL STORY AND TESTIMONY" EXERCISE

<u>Short Biography Guidelines:</u> In one paragraph answer the following: Where are you from? Brief family history (parents, siblings, spouse, and/or children). What do you do for work and play (hobbies)? Share one interesting or unknown fact about yourself.

<u>Testimony Guidelines:</u> Limit to one page written or typed.

PURPOSE: Sharing your testimony and the work God has done in your life is an invaluable tool for evangelism and relationship building. Sharing testimonies also has the ability to encourage a faith community that is suffering, broken, or doubting God. It is a personal reminder concerning the work God has already done in your life, and gives the assurance that he will finish the work he has begun in your heart. Our personal stories also reveal to us and others the life experiences that have shaped our identity and gives us a good place to start when having conversations about how we view God, ourselves, and others.

A Biblical Model: Read the following passages. Genesis 45:1-28, John 4:4–42, and 2 Corinthians. 1:3–11. What does God reveal to you about himself, and the importance of knowing our own stories?

• Authentically sharing your story gives you the opportunity to:
• Confess that we all struggle and are desperately in need of the Lord's grace and help
• Boast about the goodness and faithfulness of God
• Celebrate and rejoice in the grace of God regarding your success
• Be discerning and purposeful about the way ahead
• Learn wisdom and discernment (Everybody does not need to know everything. Prayerfully ask God how you can glorify him with this opportunity.)
• Remember that you are a part of God's story.[25]

LESSON I AGENDA

MENTOR FOR FREEDOM

Date:_____

I.   Leader Introduction:
      A. Opening Prayer (Galatians 5:13-15 Devotion *optional*)
      B. Welcome: Personal Introduction and Passion for Mentoring
      C. Share highlights from "Christian Leader as Mentor" essay

II.   Group Learning: Getting to Know You (Share short biographies and testimonies.)

III. Group Discussion: *Mentor for Life*, Chapters 1-3
      A. The Mentoring Mission
      B. Connecting Evangelism and Discipleship
      C. Challenges for Leading the Church and Culture

IV.   Mentoring Instruction: Watch "Mentor for Life" Video Lesson I: Mentor for Freedom

V.   Group Discussion Questions

VI.   Team Building/Collaborative Exercise: Mentoring Purpose, Vision, Mission, and Values

VII. Announcements

VIII. Prayer Time

Mentor Notes:

FOLLOW-UP ACTION ITEMS:

LESSON I Group Discussion Questions

A. What questions did this lesson's *Mentor for Life* reading bring to mind?

B. What were your key points of learning from this lesson's *Mentor for Life* reading?

C. What are some of your fears regarding the opportunity to lead and mentor others? How can this training opportunity and leadership team help you confront those fears?

TEAM BUILDING/COLLABORATIVE EXERCISE:
MENTORING PURPOSE, VISION, MISSION, AND VALUES

Review *Mentor for Life* Appendix C: Quick Reference Guide for Joining a Mentoring Group

Use the mentoring principles and tools shared in the *Mentor for Life* book and this training resource, and determine the best practices for your ministry context. How will you collectively answer the following questions for potential mentees:

1. What is the purpose of the mentoring group or discipleship/mentoring ministry?

2. Vision: What do you hope to accomplish by offering this mentoring opportunity? Better yet: What do you believe God wants communicated and lived in and among all participants?

3. Mission: How will you respond to God or work towards this vision? What is the mentoring process? What is the group or ministry's period of commitment? What are the core values, tools, and/or focused areas of spiritual development that will help you move towards this vision?

4. What commitments are you asking of the mentors (including yourself) and mentees?

Note: You will not complete this exercise during Lesson I. Your purpose at this time is to start thinking and working together as a team, and to prepare each other to communicate the same message when reaching out to potential mentees. The goal is to work on clarifying the answers to these questions throughout your training, and to have a one page summarized response to share with others on behalf of the ministry's leadership team by the end of your training period.

Part Two

Lesson Two:

Mentor for Joy

Mentoring Community: An Invitation to Receive the Gift
of Presence with God and with Others

Preparation for Lesson II

PERSONAL EXERCISE FOR THE LESSON: Exercise Instructions provided on next page – Complete "The Discipline of Study" Exercise.

Required Reading (Note: This material must be read prior to the team's lesson):

- *Mentor for Life: Finding Purpose Through Intentional Discipleship*, Chapters 5–6
- *Mentor for Life*, Appendix A: Richard Foster on the Inward Discipline of Study
- Article: "Retaining What You Read" by Natasha Sistrunk Robinson
- Mentoring Resource Reading: Optional

DEFINITION OF MENTORING

Mentoring is a trusted partnership where people share wisdom that fosters spiritual growth and leads to transformation, as mentors and mentees grow in their love of Christ, knowledge of self, and love of others.

PURPOSE OF THIS LESSON:

The purpose of this lesson is to help potential mentors explore the importance of theological reflection and study, and consider how presence with God and with others in Christian community can transform us and restore our joy.

OBJECTIVE

The prospective mentor will develop a foundational understanding of theological reflection and study as essential disciplines for intentional discipleship and mentoring.

GOALS

1) The prospective mentor will have a biblical understanding of the importance of renewing or training one's mind.

2.) The prospective mentor will begin to cultivate a habit of study and theological reflection.

"THE DISCIPLINE OF STUDY" EXERCISE

Read *Mentor for Life*, Appendix A: Richard Foster on the Inward Discipline of Study.

The purpose of Spiritual Disciplines is the total transformation of the person. They aim at replacing old destructive habits of thought with new life-giving habits. Nowhere is this purpose more clearly seen than in the Discipline of study.
– Richard J. Foster

"Many are hampered and confused in the spiritual walk by a simple ignorance of the truth. Worse yet, many have been brought into the most cruel bondage by false teaching."[26]

Write out the following scriptures:

Romans 12:2 –

John 8:31–32 –

Acts 17:10-11 –

2 Corinthians 10:3-5 –

What do each of these passages reveal about the importance of study?

LESSON II AGENDA

MENTOR FOR JOY

Date:_____

I.   Leader Introduction:
      A. Opening Prayer (Psalm 16 Devotion *optional*)
      B. Welcome: Personal Thoughts Concerning the Lesson
      C. Highlights: "Retaining What You Read" Article

II.   Group Learning: Review and Discuss "The Discipline of Study" exercise

III. Mentoring Instruction: Watch "Mentor for Life" Video Lesson II: Mentor for Joy

IV.   Group Discussion Questions and Time of Sharing:
      Mentor for Life, Mentoring: A Commitment to Presence, Chapters 5–6

V.   Team Building/Collaborative Exercise: Mentoring Ministry Purpose, Vision, Mission, and Values
      (Continued from Lesson I)

VI.   Announcements

VII. Prayer Time

Mentor Notes:

┌─────────────────────────────┐
│ **FOLLOW-UP ACTION ITEMS:** │
│   │
│   │
│   │
│   │
│   │
│   │
│   │
│   │
└─────────────────────────────┘

LESSON II Group Discussion Questions

Mentor for Life, Mentoring: A Commitment to Presence, Chapters 5-6

A. What are some intentional ways you can challenge your mentees to embrace the gifts of silence and solitude, and pursue the presence of God in their lives?

B. As a mentor, what ways can you welcome the gift of silence even in your mentoring community? Consider the differences between engaging introverts and extroverts with shared participation and value in a mentoring group.

C. What might God be asking you to give up or surrender to allow for this mentoring opportunity?

D. In what ways are you change or risk adverse? How might you overcome these uncertainties and fears and take the risk of mentoring others?

Part Two

Lesson Three:

Mentor for Love

Mentoring Community: An Invitation to Receive the Gift
of Presence with God and with Others

Receive God's Love. Love Other People.

#Mentor4Life

43

PERSONAL EXERCISE FOR THE LESSON: Exercise instructions provided on next page – Complete "The Affirmations for Mentoring Group" Exercise

Required Reading (Note: This material must be read prior to the team's lesson):
- *Mentor for Life*: *A Commitment to God's Mission*, Chapters 9–10
- *Mentor for Life*, Appendices D: Mentoring Covenant and E: Mentoring Affirmations
- Mentoring Resource Reading: *Optional*

DEFINITION OF MENTORING

Mentoring is a trusted partnership where people share wisdom that fosters spiritual growth and leads to transformation, as mentors and mentees grow in their love of Christ, knowledge of self, and love of others.

PURPOSE OF THIS LESSON:

The purpose of this lesson is to help potential mentors create a safe, organized, and loving mentoring environment for all.

OBJECTIVE

The prospective mentor will develop safe boundaries and healthy expectations for learning and sharing within a mentoring group.

GOALS

1) The prospective mentor will create positive affirmations for their mentoring group.

2.) The prospective mentor will set and clearly communicate expectations to encourage spiritual growth in a safe and loving learning community.

"THE AFFIRMATIONS OF MENTORING GROUP" EXERCISE

Read *Mentor for Life*, Appendix D: Mentoring Covenant and Appendix E: Affirmations.

Now that you understand the importance of the mentoring mission, and know the overall vision, mission, and core values of the mentoring ministry in your local context, it is time to establish expectations or acceptable standards for your mentoring group. Standards are established for the purpose of creating a healthy, safe, loving, and effective learning environment. These standards will be the catalyst for the development of trusting relationships within your mentoring group.

Galatians 6:1–6 NIV reads:
Brothers, if someone is caught in sin, you who are spiritual should restore him gently. But watch yourself, or you also may be tempted. Carry each other's burdens, and in this way you will fulfill the law of Christ. If anyone thinks he is something when he is nothing he deceives himself. Each one should test his own actions. Then he can take pride in himself, without comparing himself to somebody else, for each one should carry his own load. Anyone who receives instruction in the word must share all good things with his instructor.

What expectations would cultivate a mentoring group where:

- Sin is confronted and confessed, and people are restored into right fellowship with God and others?
- Each person stands on the truth of God's Word, while resisting the temptation and deceptive schemes of the enemy?
- Each person carries the burdens of others and fulfills Christ's law of love which requires us to rejoice with those who rejoice and weep with those who mourn?
- Each person grows in his or her identity in Christ, and stops comparing themselves to other people?
- Each person takes responsibility for his or her own actions? and
- Rejoice in God's truth, the ability to teach and understand this truth, and in the good news of the kingdom.

A few nuggets of assistance:

1) Keep your affirmations concise.

2) Keep your list of affirmations short (no more than 10).

3) What does the Word say about the affirmations you have outlined? Consider including scripture references.

4) Review affirmations with your mentees monthly until everyone embraces the standards.

Note: Completing and requiring the signing of a "Mentoring Covenant" is optional.

LESSON III AGENDA
MENTOR FOR LOVE

Date: _____

I. Leader Introduction:
    A. Opening Prayer (1 Corinthians 13:4-7 Devotion *optional*)
    B. Welcome: Personal Thoughts Concerning the Lesson

II. Group Learning/Discussion: Why is it important to set expectations in your mentoring group?
    What can mentees expect from you? What do you expect from them? Share mentoring group affirmations.

III. Mentoring Instruction: Watch "Mentor for Life" Video Lesson III: Mentor of Love

IV. Group Discussion Questions and Time of Sharing:
    Mentor for Life, Mentoring: A Commitment to God's Mission, Chapters 9-10

V. Team Building/Collaborative Exercise:
    A. Complete Mentoring Ministry Purpose, Vision, Mission, and Values
    B. Discuss and Decide on the "Practical Tips for Your Mentoring Group/Ministry"

VI. Announcements

VII. Prayer Time

Mentor Notes:

FOLLOW-UP ACTION ITEMS:

LESSON III Group Discussion Questions

Mentor for Life, Mentoring: A Commitment to God's Mission, Chapters 9-10

A. What were your key points of learning from this lesson's *Mentor for Life* reading?

B. As a mentor, what language will you use to communicate God's kingdom mission to mentees? How can this understanding challenge the priorities of your life and theirs?

C. How can you create a healthy mentoring environment that is mission-focused and considerate of the felt needs of others?

D. As a mentor, how can you train yourself to ask the right questions? Share some tools and resources that are available to you.

TEAM BUILDING/COLLABORATIVE EXERCISE:
PRACTICAL TIPS FOR YOUR MENTORING GROUP

1. Start on time and end on time. A typical mentoring group gathering will be monthly for a period of three hours. It is the mentor's responsibility to monitor the time throughout the group's gathering.

2. Be prepared. In addition to prayer and reviewing mentoring materials, it is also important to prepare your mind, heart, and your home to provide a welcoming space to receive mentees. Be hospitable and considerate of others.

3. Be present. Do what's necessary to eliminate distractions (i.e. everyone turn off cell phones, do not meet in a space that is frequently traveled by other family members or pets, etc.).

4. Set the tone for mutual learning and respect.

- Begin each gathering in prayer and let mentees know the focus and plan for the gathering.
- Try to get all mentees involved and active. As you progress throughout the mentoring season, give others the opportunity to pray, read scripture, or lead part of the group discussion(s). Remember, in addition to their spiritual growth and development, you are equipping them to disciple others. They will learn best by doing.
- Encourage mentees to talk about themselves and not about other people. A mentoring group is not a place for gossip, even when discussed as prayer requests.
- Don't pretend like you have all of the answers. Get comfortable saying "I don't know" and/or "I will look into this and let you know." Better yet, encourage mentees to explore the question themselves and revisit the topic at the next group gathering if appropriate.
- Do not be afraid to provide biblical correction and direction. If someone makes a statement that does not have a biblical foundation, gently ask her or him to refer to the Bible passages that guide their thinking or conclusions.

Lesson Four:

Mentor for Peace

Becoming a Peacemaker: Embracing Unity in Diversity

Preparation for Lesson IV

PERSONAL EXERCISE FOR THE LESSON: Exercise instructions provided on next page – Complete "Am I a Peacemaker?" Exercise.

Required Reading (Note: This material must be read prior to the team's lesson):
- *Mentor for Life: Finding Purpose Through Intentional Discipleship*, Chapters 11-14
- Becoming a Peacemaker Handouts
- Mentoring Resource Reading: *Optional*

DEFINITION OF MENTORING
Mentoring is a trusted partnership where people share wisdom that fosters spiritual growth and leads to transformation, as mentors and mentees grow in their love of Christ, knowledge of self, and love of others.

PURPOSE OF THIS LESSON:
The purpose of this lesson is to help potential mentors teach and model the love and peace of Christ, so their mentees can have healthy relationships and become peacemakers who love their neighbors well.

OBJECTIVE
The prospective mentor will develop a foundational understanding of what it means to embrace the gospel of peace, and to live the gospel of peace in our daily lives and relationships.

GOALS
1) The prospective mentor will have a biblical understanding of the nature of conflict and the reconciliation that is available through confession, repentance, and forgiveness.

2.) The prospective mentor will communicate a biblical understanding of unity in diversity within the body of Christ.

"AM I A PEACEMAKER?" EXERCISE

Use your own words to communicate understanding of the following scriptures:

Ephesians 4:1-3 –

Romans 12:9-18 –

Colossians 3:12-15 -

Personal Reflection - Answer the following questions:

Am I a trustworthy person? Have I developed habits of gossiping, judging, inappropriately sharing information, or criticizing others? Ask some of your closest friends to share their honest perceptions concerning your trustworthiness.

Am I a safe person? Do I have a habit of intentionally or unintentionally hurting other people? How have I maintained healthy, long-term relationships in my adult life? Why or why not? Am I helpful? How do I naturally respond when others are rejoicing or mourning?

Use your own words to communicate understanding of the following scriptures:

John 17: 20-23 –

Romans 12:9-18 -

2 Corinthians 5:14-21

Personal Reflection – Answer the following questions:

How have your upbringing, culture, and life experiences shaped the way you view people who are from a different racial, ethnic, and/or socioeconomic background?

Can you articulate specific ways your life experiences and relationships have shaped you? How do these experiences equip you to mentor a diverse group of people?

LESSON IV AGENDA
MENTOR FOR PEACE

Date:_____

I.   Leader Introduction:
      A. Opening Prayer (Romans 12:9-18 Devotion *optional*)
      B. Welcome: Personal Introduction to the Lesson

II.   Group Learning/Sharing: Highlights from "Becoming a Peacemaker" handouts.
      Mentors share reflections from "Am I a Peacemaker?" exercise.

III. Group Discussion: *Mentor for Life*, Chapters 11–14
      A. Be Your Sister's or Brother's Keeper
      B. This Makes a Family
      C. Embrace Unity in Diversity
      D. Embrace all Women

IV.   Mentoring Instruction: Watch "Mentor for Life" Video Lesson IV: Mentor for Peace

V.   Group Discussion Questions

VI.   Team Building/Collaborative Exercise: Case Study

VII. Announcements

VIII. Prayer Time

Mentor Notes:

Do not repay anyone evil for evil. Be careful to do what is right in the eyes of everybody. If it is possible, as far as it depends on you, live at peace with everyone (Rom. 12:17–18).

Recommended Resource Tool:
The Peacemaker: A Biblical Guide to Resolving Personal Conflict

FOLLOW-UP ACTION ITEMS:

BECOMING A PEACEMAKER

The Peacemaker's Pledge

As people reconciled to God by the death and resurrection of Jesus Christ, we believe that we are called to respond to conflict in a way that is remarkably different form the way the world deals with conflict (Matt. 5:9; Luke 6:27-36; Gal. 5:19-26). We also believe that conflict provides opportunities to glorify God, serve other people, and grow to be like Christ (Rom. 8:28-29; 1 Cor. 10:31-11:1; James 1:2-4). Therefore, in response to God's love and in reliance on his grace, we commit ourselves to responding to conflict according to the following principles.

GLORIFY GOD – depend on God's forgiveness, wisdom, power, and love. Seek to faithfully obey his commands. "So whatever you eat or drink or whatever you do, do it all for the glory of God (1 Cor. 10:31)."

Questions to Ponder: "How can I please and honor God in this situation?" Particularly, how can I bring praise to Jesus by showing that he has saved me and is changing me?

GET THE LOG OUT OF YOUR OWN EYE – Trust God's mercy and take responsibility for your own contribution to the conflict. Confess sins to God and those you have wronged. "You hypocrite, first take the plank out of your own eye, and then you will see clearly to remove the speck from your brother's eye" (Matt. 7:5).

Question to Ponder: "How can I show Jesus' work in me by taking responsibility for my contribution to this conflict?"

GENTLY RESTORE – Overlook minor offenses and graciously confront offenses for the purpose of restoring the relationship. "Brothers, if someone is caught in a sin, you who are spiritual should restore him gently" (Gal. 6:1).

Questions to Ponder: "How can I serve others by helping them take responsibility for their contribution to the conflict?"

GO AND BE RECONCILED – Actively pursue genuine peace and reconciliation, forgiving others as Christ has forgiven you. "Therefore, if you are offering your gift at the altar and there remember that your brother has something against you, leave your gift there in front of the altar. First go and be reconciled with your brother; then come and offer your gift" (Matt. 5:23-24).

Questions to Ponder: "How can I demonstrate the forgiveness of God and encourage a reasonable solution to this conflict?"

This handout is outlined from Ken Sande's book, The Peacemaker: A Biblical Guide to Resolving Personal Conflict (Baker Books, a division of Baker Publishing Group, copyright 2004, pages 259-261). Used by permission.

THE NATURE OF CONFLICT

For Meditation:

Peacemakers who sow in peace raise a harvest of righteousness (James 3:18).

Blessed are the peacemakers, for they will be called sons of God (Matt. 5:9).

We are called to: 1.) Trust God, 2.) Obey God, 3.) Imitate God, and 4.) Acknowledge God (31–33).

Definition:

Conflict – "a difference in opinion or purpose that frustrates someone's goals or desires."

Four primary causes of conflict (30):
1. Misunderstandings resulting from poor communication (Josh. 22:10–34)
2. Differences in values, goals, gifts, calling, priorities, expectations, interests, or opinions (Acts 15:39, 1 Cor. 12:12–31)
3. Competition over limited resources, such as time or money, is a frequent source of disputes in families, churches, and businesses (Gen. 13:1–12)
4. Sinful attitudes and habits that lead to sinful words and actions (James 4:1-2)

Take Away:
Although we should seek unity in our relationships, we should not demand uniformity (Eph. 4:1-13). Instead of avoiding all conflicts or demanding that others always agree with us, we should rejoice in the diversity of God's creation and learn to accept and work with people who simply see things differently than we do (Rom. 15:7; cf. 14:1-13).

"Conflict provides opportunities to glorify God, to serve others, and to grow to be like Christ."

This handout is outlined from Ken Sande's book, *The Peacemaker: A Biblical Guide to Resolving Personal Conflict* (Baker Books, a division of Baker Publishing Group, copyright 2004). Used by permission.

CONFLICT STARTS IN THE HEART

For Meditation:

What causes fights and quarrels among you? Don't they come from your desires that battle within you?
You want something but don't get it. You kill and covet, but you cannot have what you want.
You quarrel and fight. You do not have, because you do not ask God. When you ask, you do not receive,
because you ask with wrong motives, that you may spend what you get on your pleasures (James 4:1-3).

Jesus: "You have heard that it was said to the people long ago, 'Do not murder' and anyone who murders will be subject to judgment. But I tell you that anyone who is angry with his brother will be subject to judgment" (Matt. 5:21-22a).

Definition:

Idol – "is anything apart from God that we depend on to be happy, fulfilled, or secure. In biblical terms, it is something other than God that we set our heart on (Luke 12:29; 1 Cor. 10:19), that motivates us (1 Cor. 4:5), that masters or rules us (Ps. 119:133; Eph. 5:5), or that we trust, fear, or serve (Isa. 42:17; Matt. 6:24; Luke 12:4–5). In short, it is something we love and pursue more than God" (Phil. 3:19).

"The root cause of conflict: *unmet desires in our hearts.* When we want something and feel that we will not be satisfied unless we get it, that desire starts to control us. If others fail to meet our desires, we sometimes condemn them in our hearts and fight harder to get our own way."

> **Progression of an idol: desire → demand → judge → punish**

This handout is outlined from Ken Sande's book, *The Peacemaker: A Biblical Guide to Resolving Personal Conflict* (Baker Books, a division of Baker Publishing Group, copyright 2004). Used by permission.

FROM CONFLICT TO CONFESSION

For Meditation:

"If you really want to make peace, ask God to help you breathe grace by humbly and thoroughly admitting your wrongs."

"He who conceals his sins does not prosper, but whoever confesses and renounces them finds mercy" (Prov. 28:13).

Confession – the admission of sin and examining the roots of the sin in order to move forward to restoration and wholeness.

Seven A's of Confession

1. **A**ddress everyone involved (All those whom you affected, Ps. 32:5; 41:4)

2. **A**void if, but, and maybe (Do not try to excuse your wrongs)

3. **A**dmit specifically (Both attitudes and actions, Luke 15:21)

4. **A**cknowledge the hurt (Express sorrow for the hurt you caused)

5. **A**ccept the consequences (Where appropriate seek to make restitution, Luke 15:19)

6. **A**lter your behavior (Change your attitudes and actions)

"To acknowledge that you cannot change on your own and are depending on God, it is often helpful to begin describing your plan for change with the words, 'With God's help, I plan to…'."

7. **A**sk for forgiveness (and allow time)

"Sometimes forgiveness is inhibited because a confession was inadequate."

What do you glean from: Luke 15:11–32; Matthew 7:3–5; 1 John 1:8–9; Proverbs 28:13 –

"To be a peacemaker, you need to deal honestly with your contribution to a conflict."

This handout is outlined from Ken Sande's book, *The Peacemaker: A Biblical Guide to Resolving Personal Conflict* (Baker Books, a division of Baker Publishing Group, copyright 2004, pages 127–134). Used by permission.

REPENTANCE AND FORGIVENESS

Repentance is More Than a Feeling:

The gospel shows us how important reconciliation is to God, which inspires us to do everything we can to repair any harm we have caused to others and to be reconciled to those we have offended. This restoration process involves four activities: repentance, self-examination, confession, and personal change (118). – Ken Sande

For Meditation:

"Godly sorrow brings repentance that leads to salvation and leaves no regret, but worldly sorrow brings death" (2 Cor. 7:9-10).

"Bear with each other and forgive whatever grievance you may have against one another. Forgive as the Lord forgave you" (Col. 3:13).

Definition:

<u>Repent</u> – to change the way we think or come to our senses. It involves a change of heart that acknowledges our personal offense against God.

<u>Sin</u> – "'to miss the mark.' It may also be described as failing to be and do what God commands and doing what God forbids (1 John 3:4)…it is rebellion against God's personal desires and requirements"

Forgiveness is a Decision:

Forgiveness is an active process…Forgiveness is the opposite of excusing. The very fact that forgiveness is needed and granted indicates that what someone did was wrong and inexcusable. Forgiveness says, "We both know that what you did was wrong and without excuse. But since God has forgiven me, I forgive you."…To forgive someone means to release him or her from liability to suffer punishment or penalty. – Ken Sande

Forgiveness may be described as a decision to make four promises (20):
   "I will not dwell on this incident."
   "I will not bring up this incident again and use it against you."
   "I will not talk to others about this incident."
   "I will not let this incident stand between us or hinder our personal relationship."

What do you glean from these passages? 2 Tim. 2:24-26; Luke 15:17; Ezek. 14:6; Acts 3:19; Jer. 31:34b; Isa. 43:25; Ps. 103:3-4, 12; 1 Cor. 13:5 –

<u>Repentance</u> and <u>Forgiveness</u> lead to <u>Reconciliation</u> and living as reconciled people is what makes Christians an example to the rest of the world. Read: 2 Cor. 5:17-21 & John 17:20-23.

This handout is outlined from Ken Sande's book, *The Peacemaker: A Biblical Guide to Resolving Personal Conflict* (Baker Books, a division of Baker Publishing Group, 2004). Used by permission.

LESSON IV Group Discussion Questions
Mentor for Life, Mentoring: A Commitment to Community, Chapters 11–12
Mentor for Life, Mentoring: A Commitment to Relationships, Chapters 13–14

A. What were your key points of learning from this lesson's *Mentor for Life* reading?

B. What are some ways you can rejuvenate or encourage each other as a team and leadership community when mentoring just seems too hard?

C. Does your local church reflect the diversity of your local community? How can you use mentoring to invite the "other" into relationship?

TEAM BUILDING/COLLABORATIVE EXERCISE:
SAMPLE CASE STUDY: THE CASE OF THE MISSING MENTEE

The mentor presenting the case may choose to read the case study, while other team members read along, or the mentor may opt to role play with another team member. The latter option gives the team opportunities to discuss different scenarios as they consider resolutions to the conflict.

Background: Lisa moved to town six months ago with her young son. She is recently divorced and while she does have some family in town, the relationships are not very close. Lisa desires a fresh start. She is thankful for her new job, but is lonely and does not have any friends. She was so glad to connect with Barbara, whose boy is on Lisa's son's basketball team. Barbara is a Christian and devoted member of her church, family, and community. Barbara is also a mentor in the Women's Mentoring Ministry at her church. Lisa says she is a Christian but is having difficultly trusting God in the midst of life's most recent events. Lisa was thrilled when Barbara shared the opportunity to connect in an intimate relationship with other women of faith who are in the mentoring ministry.

Description: Lisa has been actively involved in the mentoring group for the first four months. Her mentor is Stephanie, who is ten years her senior, a wife and stay-at-home mom of three girls, and a devoted member of Barbara's church. Lisa is in a group with four other mentees, all members of Barbara's church, and everyone is busy. Over the course of the first four months, Lisa had not spent quality time with her mentor or any of the mentees outside of the context of their monthly mentoring group gathering. The ladies had a wonderful time connecting during their first month of mentoring, and discovering God together in the next three months. They are all struggling with revelations of unresolved issues that are surfacing as a result of their mentoring reading and group discussions concerning their identity in Christ. Lisa has not attended the last two months of mentoring. She is not returning Stephanie's calls or emails and Lisa is not a member of their church, so Stephanie has not seen her on Sunday mornings. Several of the mentees have reached out to Lisa with no response.

Analysis: Everyone in the mentoring group is concerned about Lisa and they long to see her return to their mentoring group. What are some of the issues observed? What is going on with the mentor? Lisa? Other members of the group? What are some options to resolving this issue?

Evaluation: Put yourself in Stephanie's position, "What would you do? Have you been effective and intentional in cultivating a personal relationship with Lisa? What can you do now to reconnect? How well do you know Lisa or her needs?" "What factors or forces emerged that you did not anticipate? What questions might the group discuss that would be most helpful to you?"[27]

Theological Reflection: Read Galatians 6:1-10. In light of this reflection, how might God lead this mentor to respond?

Lesson Five:

Mentor for Hope

**Fundamentals and Essentials of the Christian Faith:
Introduction to Spiritual Disciplines**

Perseverance. Character. Hope.

#Mentor4Life

Preparation for Lesson V

PERSONAL EXERCISE FOR THE LESSON: Provided on the next pages –
Look up the scriptures and take notes for the "Spiritual Growth" handouts.

Required Reading (Note: This material must be read prior to the team's lesson):

- *Mentor for Life: Finding Purpose Through Intentional Discipleship*, Chapters 7–8
- Mentoring Resource Reading: *Optional*

DEFINITION OF MENTORING

Mentoring is a trusted partnership where people share wisdom that fosters spiritual growth and leads to transformation, as mentors and mentees grow in their love of Christ, knowledge of self, and love of others.

PURPOSE OF THIS LESSON:

The purpose of this lesson is to ensure that potential mentors understand and can articulate the essentials of the Christian faith, practices of spiritual disciplines, and the hope we have in Christ.

OBJECTIVE

The prospective mentor will develop a foundational understanding of the Christian faith and what it means to live and mature as an eternal follower of Jesus Christ.

GOALS

1) The prospective mentor will articulate the essentials of the Christian faith.

2.) The prospective mentor will effectively apply the Word of God to the essential denominational doctrines, teachings of their church, and practice of spiritual disciplines.

Spiritual Growth: According to the Word of God
1 Timothy 4:7–8 and 15

Spiritual Death	Adoption Justification	Infant/New Life as a Child of God	Growing Child/ Learning through Teaching & Modeling	Mature Adult/ Spiritual Maturity & Continued Growth

Blind, Lost & Darkness

Descriptions of any
life apart from God

Glorification

Scripture References:

1 Corinthians 1:18	Romans 3–4	Heb. 5:13	Hebrews 6:103	1 Cor. 13:11
John 3:16–21	Romans 6	Matt. 18:1–4		Titus 2
1 Colossians 1:21–23	Romans 8	John 3:1-7		Heb. 5:11–14
2 Corinthians 7:10				

Adoption – "God's act of making otherwise estranged human beings part of God's spiritual family by including them as inheritors of the riches of divine glory. This adoption takes place through our receiving in faith the work of Jesus Christ the Son, being born of the Spirit and receiving the Spirit of adoption."[28]

Scripture References: Romans 8:12–16 and Galatians 3:26 and 4:6

Justification – "The divine act whereby God makes humans, who are sinful and therefore worthy of condemnation, acceptable before a God who is holy and righteous. More appropriately described as 'justification by grace through faith,' this key doctrine of the Reformation asserts that a sinner is justified (pardoned from the punishment and condemnation of sin) and brought into relationships with God by faith in God's grace alone."[29]

Scripture References: Galatians 3:7–8 and 13–14; Romans 3:23–26, 30, and 5:9–10; and Acts 13:38–39

Sanctification – "From the Hebrew and Greek, 'to be set apart' from common use, 'to be made holy.' The nature of sanctification is twofold in that Christians have been made holy through Christ and are called to continue to grow into and strive for holiness by cooperating with the indwelling Holy Spirit until they enjoy complete conformity to Christ (glorification)."[30]

Scripture References: Romans 8:28–29, John 17:17, Ephesians 4:17–5:21, Thessalonians 4:3–4, 7-7, & Colossians 3:1–17

Glorification – "The last stage in the process of sanctification, namely, the resurrection of the body at the second coming of Jesus Christ and the entrance into the eternal kingdom of God. In glorification believers attain complete conformity to the image and likeness of the glorified Christ and are freed from both physical and spiritual defect. Glorification ensures that believers will never again experience bodily decay, death or illness, and will never again struggle with sin."[31]

Scripture Reference: Isaiah 26:19; Matthew 24; John 5:21, 24, 28–29; 1 John 3:2–3; 1 Thessalonians 4:13–5:11; and Revalation 21:3–8

Spiritual Growth: Our Identity and Faith Journey Through Christ

Because of Who He Is...	We Are... (Our Identity in Christ)
His Righteousness Christ is the Perfect Son of God	Our Justification Believers in Christ are Made Perfect Through Him
His Cross (Road to Suffering) Hebrews 5:7-10 Isaiah 53 1 Peter 2:21-25	Our Obedience Matthew 5:10 Romans 8:17-18 1 Peter 4:12-16 and 19
His Obedience/Sinless Life 2 Corinthians 5:21 Romans 5:18-19 1 Corinthians 1:26-31 Hebrews 10:10	Our Holiness/Righteousness 1 Peter 1:13-16 2 Corinthians 7:1 Hebrews 12:14 Hebrews 10:11-18

Notes:

LESSON V AGENDA
MENTOR FOR HOPE

Date: _____

I.   Leader Introduction:
     A. Opening Prayer (1 Timothy 4:7-8 Devotion *optional*)
     B. Welcome: Personal Thoughts Concerning the Lesson

II. Group Learning and Sharing: "Spiritual Growth" Discussion

III. Mentoring Instruction: Watch "Mentor for Life" Video Lesson V: Mentor for Hope

IV. Group Discussion Questions and Time of Sharing:
     Mentor for Life, Mentoring: A Commitment to a Disciplined Life, Chapters 7-8

V.   Announcements

VI. Prayer Time

Mentor Notes:

```
FOLLOW-UP ACTION ITEMS:




```

Recommended Resource Tools:
Charts of Christian Theology and Doctrine by H. Wayne House *Dictionary of Everyday Theology and Culture*, edited by Bruce Demarest & Keith J. Matthews

A. What were your key points of learning from this lesson's *Mentor for Life* reading?

B. Is reading the Bible part of your daily routine? Now that you understand the benefits of Bible engagement, how can you practically make this discipline a priority in your life?

C. Do you regularly practice any spiritual disciplines? If so, how have they contributed to your spiritual transformation? If not, what has hindered your ability to embrace a spiritual discipline?

D. As a mentor, how can you share and encourage mentees regarding essential teachings of the faith and spiritual disciplines throughout the mentoring season?

Lesson Six:

Mentor for Life

Commissioned to Serve in God's Kingdom: Mission, Mentoring, and Multiplying

Welcome and Value the "Stranger."
We are Known and Loved.

#Mentor4Life

PERSONAL EXERCISE FOR THE LESSON: Exercise instructions on next page –
Complete the "Mentoring Across Generations" Exercise
Complete "Love" Exercise from *Mentor for Life*, Chapter 15

Required Reading (Note: This material must be read prior to the team's lesson):
* *Mentor for Life: Finding Purpose Through Intentional Discipleship*, Chapters 4, 15–16
* Review "Christians in the World: Mission, Mentoring, and Multiplying" material
* Mentoring Resource Reading: *Optional*

DEFINITION OF MENTORING
Mentoring is a trusted partnership where people share wisdom that fosters spiritual growth and leads to transformation, as mentors and mentees grow in their love of Christ, knowledge of self, and love of others.

PURPOSE OF THIS LESSON:
The purpose of this lesson is to commission mentors to serve a diverse small group of mentees, and equip them to think theologically, develop a Christian worldview, and mentor for life.

OBJECTIVE
The prospective mentor will learn the general differences between generations, and prepare themselves and others to mentor for life in light of the changing culture in the world and church.

GOALS
1) The prospective mentor will apply mentoring training lessons to serve a diverse group of mentees who know and love God, understand their identity in Christ, and love their neighbors.

2.) The prospective mentor will effectively apply the Word of God to cultivate a safe and loving learning community that fosters spiritual growth and intimate relationships in the body of Christ.

MENTORING ACROSS GENERATIONS

Generations & Their Differences[32]

Generations	The Builder Generation or Traditionalists (born before 1945)	The Boomer Generation (born between 1946-1965)	The Buster Generation or Generation X (born between 1965-1983)	The Bridger Generation or Millennials (Born between 1984-Present)
Generational Identity Markers	Survivors, Strivers, Seniors, Stability	Transformational, Educated professionals, Working with no kids at home (maybe raising grandkids), political activist (Women & Civil Rights), The "Me" Generation	Individualistic, free-dom-minded, entrepre-neurial	Diversity, collaborative, determined, polite, tolerant, internet generation
Formative Life Experiences	World War I & II (in-cluding Pearl Harbor), Great Depression, "Leave It to Beaver" family model (rural communities)	Television, Economic Affluence, Education & Technology, Civil Rights Movement, Rock-n-roll	Roe vs. Wade, technol-ogy, video games, tele-vision, AIDS, Clinton administration	September 11th (911)/ter-rorist attacks, MTV, Obama administration, "Reality" television, "Modern" family
Community Focus	Family, School, and Church	Media-oriented, Working environment (workaholics), fitness communities, connect through hobbies	Latchkey kids, Free-dom, feel neglected and lonely, willing to work, reject Boomer vales, desire practical education	Desire for connection & interactivity (social media), accepting of others, close to parents & grandparents
Characteristics & Values	Hard workers, Patri-otic, Financial Savers, Loyal (follow the Chain of Command), Private (less likely to share/be authentic), respectful, accountabil-ity, dependable/stable, intolerant, courteous	Educated, Activists, question authority, inde-pendent, Competitive	postponing marriage, shorter attention span, want up-to-date infor-mation (tech savvy)	Fast-paced living, Live and let live, entrepreneurial, interactive, demanding, diverse & tolerant, asking questions
Religious Characteristics	Committed to church, support foreign mis-sions, loyal to denomi-nations	Committed to relation-ships, Supportive, toler-ant of differences	Committed to family, desire to connect faith w/ work	Committed to a group, spirituality, desire honest relationships & authentic faith
Ministry	Group activities, mis-sion projects, in-depth Bible study, Sunday School, focus on mar-riage and family	Offer multiple options, use small groups, ex-pand roles for women, focus on local ministry (normally w/ short-term ministry involvement), spiritually searching	Focus on local issues, small groups	Holistic discipleship, model authentic faith, use technol-ogy, biblical tolerance & acceptance, include women in leadership
Common Needs, Con-cerns, & Interests	Retirement/financial concerns, affordable housing, personal safety, declining health, adequate transporta-tion, preparation for death	Desire to return to traditional values, slower lifestyle, midlife transitions, death of the American Dream	Sports & fitness, friends & family, entertainment & music, the environ-ment	Easily bored, technology (gadgets), honest & open talk

<u>Avoid Generational Myths & Conflicts:</u>

- While it is important to understand the differences between generations and how the culture and historic experiences have shaped people over time, avoid referring to individuals in another generation as a collective "they." Individuals in your mentoring group may not fit the mold of all the characteristics concerning their generation.
- Do not assume that people from another generation (younger or older) have nothing to offer. The age of the mentor (or mentee) must not be a point of contention or division. What does matter is the spiritual maturity, sincerity, passion, and contributions to the mentoring group, and how God has divinely placed each of you together for a purpose.
- Likewise, do not assume that because of differences or a lack of knowledge that you have nothing to offer. Mentoring is a mutually beneficial and learning opportunity. As you share your life and story, connect the personal lessons learned with the present conversation and similar connections from other generations.

What Does the Bible say about Generations?

God cares about his name being proclaimed across generations. Take note of these verses:

Deut. 6:1-10 –

Judges 2:10 –

Titus 2 –

I Timothy 4:11-16 –

Mentoring a cross generational lines gives us the opportunity to intentionally pursue unity and reconciliation across generations, and break the yokes of historical sin in the body of Christ.

Throughout the Old Testament, God regularly refers to himself as the "God of Abraham, Isaac, and Jacob."
God cares about his name being proclaimed across generations.
– Natasha Sistrunk Robinson

CHRISTIAN WORLDVIEW:

HOW DO WE SHARE AN UNCHANGING BIBLICAL TRUTH IN A CHANGING WORLD?

The Bible

MENTORING:

The Bridge

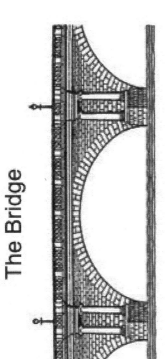

The World

- God's Absolute Truth
- Jesus ~ Life and Maturity
- Global Reach
- Defines Right Relationships

Communication & Application

- Relativism
- Lost/Broken
- Sin City
- Me-ism

Romans 1:14, 16-17 NIV:

I am obligated both to the Greeks and non-Greeks, both to the wise and the foolish…I am not ashamed of the gospel, because it is the power of God for the salvation of everyone who believes: first for the Jew, then for the Gentile. For in the gospel a righteousness from God is revealed, a righteousness that is by faith from first to last, just as it is written: "The righteous will live by faith."

1

71

REVELATION 21 22

THE WORLD IS CHANGING

"Worldwide, people are giving their lives to Jesus at an astounding rate…[yet] we are not seeing the same rate of Christian growth in the United States…At the same time, demographic shifts are changing the landscape of the United States, and the implications of these changes for American society and the church are significant…Clearly **Christians must become interculturally competent** if they are to cross the divides of age, gender, ethnicity, race, class, social status and religion in order to share the gospel."

Brenda Salter McNiel, *A Credible Witness: Reflections on Power, Evangelism and Race* *(Downers Grove, IL: IVP Books, 2008, pages 18-19)*

What is the Mentor's responsibility? How is the Church to Respond?

Live the Gospel: God's Ideal ⟶ Our Future Hope

"The job of the church is not to adopt the culture, or to merely assess and analyze the culture, but to set heaven within the context of culture so that culture can see God at work in the midst of the conflicts of men." Dr. Tony Evans, *Oneness Embraced: A Fresh Look at Reconciliation, The Kingdom, and Justice (Chicago, Moody Publishers, 2011, page 252)*

GENESIS 1 2

MENTORING IN THE WORLD: WHAT DOES IT MEAN TO BE MISSIONAL?

> "The gospel is not just about what we preach and teach; it is also about how we live with integrity in the midst of a lost and dying world."
> *Natasha Sistrunk Robinson*

IDOLTOROUS
WAYS OF THE WORLD

Materialism (Matt 6:21, 24)

Selfishness (Mark 8:34-38)

Lover of Self (2 Tim 3:2-5)

Family & Children

(Luke 14:26)

"You are the salt of the earth. But if the salt loses its saltiness, **how can it be made salty again?** It is no longer good for anything, except to be thrown out & trampled by men. "You are the light of the world. A city on a hill cannot be hidden. Neither do people light a lamp and put it under a bowl. Instead they put it on its stand, and it gives light to everyone in the house. In the same way, let your light shine before men, that they may see your good deeds and praise your Father in heaven." Matthew 5:13-16 NIV

Jesus: "While I am in the world, I am the light of the world." John 9:5

#Mentor4Life   www.natashasrobinson.com

LESSON VI AGENDA
MENTOR FOR LIFE

Date:_____

I.   Leader Introduction:
        A. Opening Prayer (John 15 Devotion *optional*)
        B. Welcome: Personal Thoughts Concerning the Lesson

II.   Group Sharing/Team Building: Share "Love" Exercise

III.   Mentoring Instruction: Watch "Mentor for Life" Video Lesson VI: Mentor for Life
        Christians in the World: Mission, Mentoring, and Multiplying

IV.   Group Discussion Questions:
        Mentoring Across Generations
        Mentor for Life, Multiplying the Kingdom and the Priesthood, Chapter 4
        Mentor for Life, Mentoring: A Commitment to Love, Chapters 15–16

V.   Announcements

VI.   Prayer Time

Mentor Notes:

FOLLOW-UP ACTION ITEMS:

LESSON VI Group Discussion Questions
Mentoring Across Generations
Mentor for Life, Multiplying the Kingdom and the Priesthood, Chapter 4
Mentor for Life, Mentoring: A Commitment to Love, Chapters 15–16

A. What generations are represented in your church? Are each of these generations represented on the mentoring leadership team? How can you intentionally connect with people from other generations through this mentoring ministry?

B. What are some ways culture has shaped your generation? What makes you proud about your generation? Who do you identify as the leaders (national and international, Christian and non-Christian) of your generation? Why?

C. What frustrates you most about your generation or other generations? Can you name any generational conflict(s) in the universal church or your local congregation?

D. How can this awareness help you better connect with and serve people from different generations within your mentoring group? What can the leadership team do to address these generational expectations, challenges and concerns?

E. What is your natural inclination and responses to "weak links" in the Body of Christ? As you prepare to mentor, how can you respond with both grace and truth to those at various stages of their faith journeys?

F. How will you intentionally speak the truth in love and share a positive vision for mentees to understand God's good gospel and his best for his children, your sisters and brothers in Christ?

G. What questions do you still have about mentoring as intentional discipleship? What more do you need to get started?

Mock Session:

Mentoring Group Practice

MOCK SESSION: MENTORING GROUP PRACTICE

PERSONAL EXERCISE FOR THE LESSON:

Complete book-net (reference appendices) for mentoring book resource #1. Complete Scripture memorization.

Required Reading (Note: This resource must be read in its entirety to the mock session):

• Mentoring Book Resource #1 Reading: _____

WHAT TO BRING

Bible, mentoring book resource, leadership training binder, book net-out,[33] writing utensil

DEFINITION OF MENTORING

Mentoring is a trusted partnership where people share wisdom that fosters spiritual growth and leads to transformation, as mentors and mentees grow in their love of Christ, knowledge of self, and love of others.

PURPOSE OF THIS LESSON:

The purpose of the mock session is to give mentors the opportunity to experience a mentoring group gathering, as one team member gains confidence in facilitating a mentoring group. The mock session(s) also provide leadership opportunities to grow closer as friends and teammates.

OBJECTIVE

All mentors will learn the skills necessary for leading their own mentoring groups.

GOALS

1.) The mentor will gain confidence in leading a mentoring small group session.

2.) The leadership team will observe, participate and document the leadership opportunities and challenges of a mentoring small group gathering.

For the mentor leading the mock mentoring session.

Mock Session Preparation

Greetings Mentor,

I want to offer a few points of consideration when preparing for the mock session:

Notice the identified differences between your leadership team and your future mentoring group:

- The mentoring leadership team may be significantly larger than your actual mentoring group.
- The mentoring leadership team generally meets for two hours. Unless otherwise communicated, your actual mentoring group will meet monthly for three hour gatherings.

Given these identified differences: monitor the time:

- There is no way to completely cover all of the mentoring elements within the allotted training time. In the mock session, make the effort to at least touch on each element, with the understanding that you will not be able to finish everything.
- Pay attention to what is happening in the room: Listening and watching are very important communication and leadership skills. Be intentional about engaging all mentors in the group conversations.
- Hospitality: On the day of the mock session, it is your responsibility to serve the leadership team.
- Prayer: Pray in preparation of the mock session, and encourage all team members to use the appropriate appendix form to document prayers shared during the mock session.

Blessings,

Natasha

MENTORING GROUP GATHERING GUIDE

In no particular order, each mentoring group gathering will consist of the following:

Food and Fellowship.

Time of Sharing. This time focuses on the mentor/mentees heart condition and includes reflections on what God is revealing to them through mentoring. This is also the time when mentors and mentees share from their journals, book net-out summaries,[34] and/or other spiritual disciplines or transformative exercises.

Scripture Memorization. Each mentor and mentee will recite the passages from the current month and as time permits review scriptures from the previous months.

Mentoring Resource Discussion. This is not a book discussion. The purpose is not to rehearse what the author said and whether or not you agreed with him or her. The purpose is to use the available tools to study the mentoring resource; reflect and evaluate the scripture references provided in the mentoring resource; and then share your personal responses of how God is using the mentoring resource in your life and what he is teaching you through the mentoring process.

Prayer and Intercession. Each person is allowed to share one prayer request per month.[35] Shared prayer requests are recorded by each mentee, along with a scripture reference to accompany the prayer. After sharing, the mentoring group must take time to intercede for each other.

★ Mentors and Mentees are expected to bring the following items to each mentoring group gathering: Bible; mentoring book resource; writing utensil; binder, journal or other recording device for note taking and prayer requests; and any "place of conversion" exercises.

MOCK SESSION: MENTORING GROUP GATHERING

Mentor: _____

Date: _____

I.   Opening Prayer & Fellowship

II.   Scripture Memorization

        Old Testament: _____

        New Testament: _____

III.   Group Discussion : mentoring resource, book net-out sharing, & practical application

IV.   Sharing of journaling, exercises, etc.

V.   Announcements, expectations, and preparation for the next group gathering

VI.   Sharing of Prayer Requests & Time of Intercession

For the Ministry Leader:

Preparation Notes

PREPARATION NOTES FOR THE MINISTRY LEADER
BEFORE YOU GET STARTED

<u>Preparation for this Training:</u>

1. Communication is Key: Remember that the idea of leading, mentoring or intentionally making disciples may be a foreign concept to the majority of your team. I cannot overstress the importance of communicating clearly and reinforcing key teaching, learning, and preparation points throughout the training and mentoring season. Use the internet, social media, or other communication tools to take advantage of this tip even when you are not gathering face-to-face.

2. For Training and Reference: This training resource serves two purposes: 1.) it provides training and documentation for your leadership team, and 2.) it is a reference tool for mentors as they prepare for their own mentoring groups. I recommend that you print this material and place it in a binder so each team member can add pertinent content throughout the mentoring season.

3. Training Time: Each lesson is scheduled to cover a two hour time period. Consider beforehand the best use of this allotted time: large group vs. small group discussion; fellowship, relationship, and team building vs. teaching and learning time; individual verses group needs; and time for practical application verses spiritual formation or soul care (incorporating spiritual disciplines).

You will learn this balance as you continue throughout the leadership training, and this is your opportunity to model for the potential mentors who themselves will have to learn the same time management skills to effectively lead their own mentoring groups.

4. *Mentor for Life*: You might notice in the training resource that the chapters from the book are not covered in order. I recommend that the entire leadership team reads *Mentor for Life* prior to beginning leadership training. In this way, everyone has the same context at the beginning of training. By the time prospective mentors begin leadership training, the *Mentor for Life* reading will actually be a study review that reinforces their learning and understanding.

5. Pace Yourself and Your Team: Six lessons does not necessarily equate to six weeks. Some of the lessons are longer than others, and it might be beneficial to divide them into two different lessons based on your ministry context, team needs, or other opportunities or teaching points you want to incorporate. The important thing is that you want the team to "get it," so allow an appropriate amount of time between your leadership team gatherings for the prospective mentors to both reflect on the last lesson and adequately to prepare for the next lesson. (I would recommend having training every other week until you have worked through all the lessons.)

Additionally, it is good practice to reinforce key points from the lessons with the team throughout the mentoring season.

6. Answer the Questions: There will be questions as you advance through this training curriculum and that is a good thing. Do not, however, allow questions to become a distraction during the training time. Address the pertinent questions as you are able within the allotted time, while allowing sufficient opportunities for team building and group discussion. Document the "off topic" questions to address at other appropriate points in the training curriculum.

Ask the Right Questions: Constantly ask yourself, "What do they need to know? What am I asking them to do? How am I connecting these two points, and setting them up for success?"

7. By the time the team begins leadership training, you should have some idea of the three mentoring resources:

Resource #1. Knowing and Loving God, Resource #2. Understanding Your Identity in Christ, and Resource #3.) Loving Your Neighbor, you intend to use during the mentoring season. These resources should be shared with the leadership team as soon as possible so they can began reading the resources. Together, decide on a reasonable timeline for the leadership team to complete the reading of those resources. Ideally, you want to have at least the first resource completed by the end of your leadership training to effectively hold a mock mentoring small group session with the leadership team.

8. Mock Session(s): At the end of the leadership training, I recommend having at least one mentoring group mock session. If your leadership team is large, you might want to split them into separate mock group sessions for the training, and then have each group share their learning during a follow-up leadership team meeting. This gives the leadership team an opportunity to model an actual mentoring small group gathering experience. I have provided instructions to assist with this practice. If you decide to have more than one mock session, allow a different mentor to lead each time. (You must not lead any of these, as this is a training opportunity for the future mentors. Preferably, you want to give this opportunity to a mentor who has not led a small group or Bible study previously.)

Now let's get started!

FOR THE LEADER: LESSON I

Preparation for the Lesson: Be prepared to:

1. Encourage and be hospitable to the team.

2. Be hospitable: Offer refreshments. Team training is your opportunity to serve the team.

3. Answer important questions during the introduction of the lesson: What can the team expect from you? What reasonable expectations can they have of each other? What can they expect to get out of training? The big picture lets them know where you are taking them (begin with the end in mind) and the small picture helps them understand where you will focus right now and how that connects to the overall big picture. COMMUNICATION IS KEY!

During the Lesson: Be prepared to:

1. Be respectful of people's time. Begin on time and end on time.

 2. Keep everyone on task. Document pertinent questions raised.

The Agenda:

1. Training Time: Each lesson is scheduled to cover a two hour time period. Consider beforehand about the best use of the time between large group and small group discussion, fellowship and relationship building, individual verses group needs, teaching and instruction time to fill gaps in learning, providing teaching opportunities for prospective mentors, and prayer.

2. Group Time: A significant amount of Lesson I is reserved for group discussion. It is important to allow everyone an opportunity to share their short biographies and testimonies. Depending on the size of the team, you may not be able to answer the "Group Discussion Questions" in this lesson and that is okay. Your primary purpose for this lesson is to ensure that the team gets to know each other and are clear concerning expectations. Document team members' questions so they are adequately addressed throughout your training lessons.

3. Announcements: Remind participants of your next training date, preparations, and mentoring lesson. Share any other pertinent information regarding the mentoring training schedule.

4. Prayer Time: During prayer time, allow each team member to share one prayer request (document in prayer log included in Appendix A). (Encourage them to be succinct in their sharing. You do not want to spend more time sharing than you do actually praying.) Ask a volunteer(s) to pray over the shared requests. For this lesson, you might also encourage participants to share the names of the persons God has placed on their heart to potentially mentor, and ask a different volunteer to pray over these potential mentees. Finally, it is always appropriate to close with a prayer of praise and thanksgiving for your time together, and petition the Lord concerning the ministry and his leadership team.

FOR THE LEADER: LESSON II

Preparation for the Lesson: Be prepared to:

1. Encourage and be hospitable to the team.

2. Offer light refreshments. Training time is your opportunity to edify and serve the team.

3. Answer important questions during the introduction of the lesson: Be sure to strategically address previous questions raised by team members, and reinforce important answers previously given. Remind them of where the team and ministry is headed together. The big picture lets them know where you are taking them (begin with the end in mind) and the small picture helps them understand where you will focus right now and how that contributes to the overall big picture. COMMUNICATION IS KEY! Tell them, tell them, and tell them again.

During the Lesson: Be prepared to:

1. Be respectful of people's time. Begin on time and end on time.

 2. Keep everyone on task. Document pertinent questions raised.

The Agenda:

1. Training Time: Each lesson is scheduled to cover a two hour time period. Consider beforehand about the best use of the time between large group and small group discussion, fellowship and relationship building, individual verses group needs, teaching and instruction time to fill gaps in learning, providing teaching opportunities for prospective mentors, and prayer.

2. Group Exercise/Learning Time: As the ministry leader, it is your responsibility to communicate the why and how for the mentor's preparation and learning.

If you have not already done so, this is an opportune time to introduce the mentoring resources you are recommending for the mentoring season:

Ministry Framework	Book Resource
Knowing and Loving God	
Knowing my Identity in Christ Jesus	
Loving My Neighbors as Myself	

Mentoring for life is a mutually beneficial experience for both the mentor and mentee. I trust that mentors will grow in their faith as they prepare to lead their mentoring groups. By renewing their minds and through the discipline of study, they will learn to think theologically, develop a Christian worldview, reject the lies of the evil one, and replace those lies with God's truth.

The practical application for mentoring concerning Richard Foster's 4 Steps of Study are:

Repetition – Mentors are expected to read the entire mentoring resources and share their book net-outs with the mentoring leadership team prior to reviewing the mentoring resources in their mentoring groups. In this way, mentors end up reviewing their mentoring resources at least three times (once on their own, once when sharing with their mentoring leadership training, and then again when teaching or facilitating their mentoring group discussion).

Concentration – The selection of mentoring resources is critically important.[36] It is important to understand your ministry context, along with the spiritual condition and needs of the mentees you are serving. Prayerfully select resources that will challenge but not overwhelm the ministry participants. Understanding that everyone in the mentoring ministry/group are at different places on their spiritual journey, your mentoring resources should in some way challenge all group participants. Learning together can be a wonderful opportunity for peer-to-peer mentoring.

Comprehension – The purposes of discussing the mentoring resources with the mentoring leadership team and in the mentoring group is to encourage dialog and increase understanding among mentors and mentees.

Reflection – After reading a mentoring resource, all mentoring group participants complete a "book net-out."[37] The book net-out is a one-page document that encourages theological and personal reflection concerning the mentoring ministry resource and studied material.

3. Announcements: Remind participants of your next training lesson, and how they can best prepare for that lesson. Share pertinent information regarding the mentoring training schedule.

4. Prayer Time: During prayer time, allow each team member to share one prayer request (document in prayer log included in Appendix A). Ask a volunteer(s) to pray over the shared requests. Close with a prayer of praise and thanksgiving for your time together, and petition the Lord concerning the ministry and its leadership team.

FOR THE LEADER: LESSON III

Preparation for the Lesson: Be prepared to:

Answer important questions during the introduction of the lesson. Be sure to strategically address previous questions raised by team members, and reinforce important answers previously given. Remind them of where the team and ministry is headed together. The big picture lets them know where you are taking them (begin with the end in mind) and the small picture helps them understand where you will focus right now and how that contributes to the overall big picture. COMMUNICATION IS KEY! Tell them, tell them, and tell them again.

The Agenda:

1. Training Time: Each lesson is scheduled to cover a two hour time period. Consider beforehand about the best use of the time between large group and small group discussion, fellowship and relationship building, individual verses group needs, teaching and instruction time to fill gaps in learning, providing teaching opportunities for prospective mentors, and prayer.

2. Team Building/Collaborative Exercise:

This is the lesson to complete your mentoring ministry purpose, vision, mission, and values. This foundational information will guide mentors throughout the rest of the mentoring season.

Throughout this lesson, help mentors think about practical tips to effectively lead their mentoring groups. Here are few key ingredients:

A. *Mentoring is intentional.* When Jesus called his disciples, his command was simple, leave everything and "Follow me." Discipleship is for those who are willing to follow and obey Jesus. Mentoring consistently challenges both mentor and mentees alike to keep Christ as our focus.

B. *Mentoring is sacrificial.* Mentoring requires commitment and mutual submission. The group expectations are the same for everyone. It communicates love and respect for God and your sisters when you are fully present, prepared, and engaged during each mentoring gathering.

C. *Mentoring is relational.* Mentoring cultivates intimate relationships of trust and accountability. The purpose of mentoring within the context of a small group is to cultivate relationships in community through a longer commitment (ideally 10-12 months).

D. *Mentoring is practical.* The purpose of mentoring in the small group context is to make disciples of Christ. This does not mean that we ignore the need for mentorship in other practical life areas. Always encourage practical learning and other connection points among participants.

3. Announcements: Remind participants of your next training lesson, and how they can best prepare for that lesson. Share pertinent information regarding the mentoring schedule.

4. Prayer Time: During prayer time, allow each team member to share one prayer request (document in prayer log included in Appendix A).

FOR THE LEADER: LESSON IV

Note: This lesson covers a lot of material, both in the reading preparation or review, and in the discussion and learning opportunities. Depending on the size and progress of your leadership team, you may opt to divide this lesson into two separate training sessions.

<u>Preparation for the Lesson:</u> Be prepared to:

1. Encourage and be hospitable to the team.

2. Offer light refreshments. Training time is your opportunity to edify and serve the team.

3. Answer important questions during the introduction of the lesson. The big picture lets them know where you are going (begin with the end in mind), and the small picture helps them understand where you will focus your attention right now and how that focus contributes to the overall big picture. COMMUNICATION IS KEY! Tell them, tell them, and tell them again.

<u>During the Lesson:</u> Be prepared to:

1. Be respectful of people's time. Begin on time and end on time.

2. Keep everyone on task.

3. Document pertinent questions and answer questions from the previous lesson(s).

<u>The Agenda:</u>

1. The Lessons concerning confession, repentance, forgiveness, and peacemaking can be reviewed with the team

throughout the mentoring season. For now, encourage reading of the provided material and discuss highlights with the group. The use of case studies and/or the sharing of personal life lessons learned are powerful ways to reinforce these teaching points.

For this lesson, invest most of this time on role play with the provided case study.

2. Announcements: Remind participants of your next training lesson, and how they can best prepare for that lesson. Share pertinent information regarding the mentoring training schedule.

3. Prayer Time: During prayer time, allow each team member to share one prayer request (document in prayer log included in Appendix A). Ask a volunteer(s) to pray over the shared requests. Close with a prayer of praise and thanksgiving for your time together, and petition the Lord concerning the ministry and its leadership team.

FOR THE LEADER: LESSON V

Preparation for the Lesson: Be prepared to:

1. Before this lesson, have a discussion with your church leadership. Since the priority for essential teachings of the faith may vary between denominations, I recommend that you consul with your church leaders and seek their wisdom for appropriate supplemental reading materials for this lesson. They can help you familiarize yourself with fundamental doctrines (or right teachings). Do not assume the prospective mentors know this important information. Some may have never considered or learned it. Now is your opportunity to teach them.

Here are some points or topics of consideration:

FUNDAMENTALS OF THE CHRISTIAN FAITH
- The Trinity (Father, Son, and Holy Spirit as One God)
- Jesus alone as Savior of the world (The nature/person and work of Christ)
- The Holy Bible (inspired by the Holy Spirit, the truth & purpose of God's Word)
- What is salvation? Who can be saved? What does salvation mean for the lost, and in the life of the believer?

TEACHINGS AND DOCTRINES OF THE CHRISTIAN FAITH
- The Nature of Human Kind and Sin
- Spiritual Dimensions (The Holy Spirit, Heaven/Hell, Satan & Evil, Angels & Demons)
- The Doctrines of Justification, Adoption, Sanctification, & Glorification
- Doctrine of the Church (What is its nature and purpose?)
- Evangelism and Discipleship

STATEMENTS OF FAITH FROM CHURCH HISTORY
- The Nicene Creed (About AD 325)
- The Apostle's Creed (About AD 390)

2. Review: This is important material to discuss during the lesson and throughout the mentoring season. Help mentors incorporate these fundamental teachings in their mentoring small groups.

The Agenda:

1. The spiritual disciplines material is covered in *Mentor for Life* Chapters 7-8. Lead the group in discussing which spiritual disciplines to implement in your ministry context. How might you implement these disciplines on your leadership team and/or in your mentoring small groups?

2. Announcements: Remind participants of your next training lesson, and how they can best prepare for that lesson. Share pertinent information regarding the mentoring training schedule.

3. Prayer Time: During prayer time, allow each team member to share one prayer request (document in prayer log included in Appendix A).

FOR THE LEADER: LESSON VI

Preparation for the Lesson: Be prepared to:

1. Make this a time of celebration and encouragement.

2. Be very clear about the next steps: When will the ministry actually launch? What needs to happen between now and then? When will the mentoring small groups begin gathering? How will you identify or connect with potential mentees? How will you connect committed mentors and those desiring to commit to a mentoring group? When is the next time and how often will you have leadership meetings to "check-in" or encourage the mentoring team and discuss their group's progress? What will be your communication plan going forward?

3. Answer important questions: What can the team expect from you going forward? What reasonable expectations can they have of each other? What do you expect from them?

4. By now, prospective mentors would have made a decision as to whether or not they will lead a mentoring small group, participate in a mentoring group, and/or remain in a supportive role. Let everyone who has completed training know who is doing what.

5. Determine and communicate how the leadership team will progress through your three mentoring resources for the season. It is important that all mentors read the material and discuss with the leadership team in advance of their mentoring small group discussions of the material.

During the Lesson: Be prepared to:

1. Remind the team of what all they have learned and readily encourage them that they are indeed ready to mentor for life.

 2. Document pertinent questions and answer questions from the previous lesson(s).

The Agenda:

1. Announcements: Remind participants of your next training lesson, and how they can best prepare for that lesson. Will you complete mock mentoring small group session(s) with the leadership team? How many? Who will lead each? When will they be held?

2. Share pertinent information regarding the leadership team and mentoring schedule.

4. Prayer Time: During prayer time, allow each team member to share one prayer request (document in prayer log included in Appendix A).

Appendices:

Prayer Request Log

Getting Started: Mentoring Ministry Checklist

Book Net-Out Instructions and Sample

The Gift of Hospitality

APPENDICES
Appendix A
LESSON _____ PRAYER REQUESTS

Date	Prayer Requests (include name)	Accompanying Scripture for Prayer	Date	Answer to Prayer

APPENDIX B
GETTING STARTED
Mentoring Ministry Checklist

❏   Train potential mentors & confirm their 1-year commitment to the ministry (10 months of mentoring and 2 months of Sabbaths rest)

❏   Determine your leadership meeting dates (Be consistent and plan ahead. Put your leadership meetings on the calendar for the entire year so mentors have this information handy when planning their mentoring group gathering dates with mentees.)

❏   Pick an official launch date

❏   Review and select the curriculum (3 Mentoring Resources) to review with the ministry team

❏   Spread the Word: Share the message (purpose, vision, mission, & values) of the ministry

❏   Invite others to join in (Mentors must first articulate their days and times of availability to lead a mentoring group. Once they have done so, please review this information with the entire mentoring team to ensure you are offering a variety of times, days, and geographical locations for potential mentees and for the community you are called to serve. Once the team agrees to the times, days, and location offering, you are prepared to offer mentoring group opportunities to potential mentees. How will you give people the opportunity to commit to a mentoring group?)

❏   Connect mentors and mentees as soon as possible after mentees have expressed interest and have completed a mentoring information form.

APPENDIX C
BOOK NET-OUT INSTRUCTIONS & SAMPLE

The Book Net-Out is a <u>one</u> page document that includes the following information:

• Name and Author of the mentoring resource (book)

• Names of the Mentor and Mentee

• Mentoring Group Gathering Date

• A Quick Summary (2-5 sentences) of the entire book

• Key Insights. Note: Key insights serve the purpose of theological reflection and personal study. Mentees must be required to think about the material. They must not simply include direct quotes from the book. Key insights consist of a summary of the reader's learning, personal take-aways, or questions they may still have. Encourage mentees to use their own words. Either a paragraph or bullet-form is sufficient. Ask mentors and mentees to ponder: What did you learn from the reading? Why does it matter? Why is this material important for you to know? How does it apply to your life, church, work, family, relationships, and community?

• Personal Application (consists of only one goal the mentor/mentee will set as a result of reading this material. This goal can be a SMART goal. It can be a critical discussion point or means of accountability within the mentoring group.)

Is your goal **Specific**? Consider: How do you describe the "goal"? What is it?

Is your goal **Measurable**? Consider: How do you define and identify success with this goal?

Is your goal **Achievable**? All things considered, is this goal realistic? What would progression towards achieving this goal look like?

Is your goal **Relevant**? Consider: How and why is this goal important at this stage of your life and spiritual journey?

Is your goal **Timely**? Consider: Is there a time or other limitation on this goal? When will you begin? When would you like to complete this goal?

BOOK NET OUT SAMPLE

She Did What She Could
Elisa Morgan (Tyndale House, 2009)

Mentor Name: Natasha Sistrunk Robinson   Date: _____

Quick Summary

Too often in the Christian faith, we paralyze ourselves because we are overwhelmed with life's circumstances or the work that is before us. Jesus has not asked us to save the world. He acknowledges our simple acts of faith. Each of us can consider what we have in our own hands, and do what we are uniquely gifted and qualified to do. Being willing vessels and offering our simple acts of obedience brings honor to God and acknowledges his presence in our lives.

Key Insights

- So much of this book answers the question of the two greatest commandments for me: "Love God" and "love my neighbor." This book calls for that love to be realized. Caring is not enough. Love must be evident in our actions. The whole of the gospel is to live loved.
- Am I compelled enough by God's love for me? Am I generous in sharing the same love I have received with others? "God's love changes us. Radically. All of us. And when we are different, we make a difference in our world…Jesus paired the gospel with a relationship of love that expresses itself in loving service."
- Page 42- The List of "I Am" statements really spoke to me. I know who I am in Christ Jesus. The gospel is about God using fallen, unworthy, sinners to lovingly carry out his good purposes in the world. Scripture review – Romans 8:28-29.
- I cannot and should not do everything I want to do or everything someone else asks me to do. I need to be clear about investing my gifts and talents in the work uniquely outlined for me.
- Be a willing vessel: "I gave me to the ministry and watched God make me enough." This statement is one of humility (not thinking of myself more highly than I ought), surrender, and trust.
- Note to self: "There is a sacrificial element to doing what you can."
- "What if I lived each day with the commitment to do what I could in that day, to know that I am loved by Jesus and to love him back?"
- I must be about God's Kingdom building agenda, and reject the futile attempts of building my own kingdom. There is great joy in kingdom—building work with other believers and watching God move among us! "This is the body of Christ in action—uniquely called to both an individual and a corporate investment of who we are."

Personal Application

I will begin each day listening to God and allowing him to speak to my heart through Bible study and prayer. I will make a note of this time to reflect monthly on reoccurring themes and messages God is speaking to my heart. This is an important discipline because I am tempted to go my own way, and make decisions without consulting God.

APPENDIX D

THE GIFT OF Hospitality

- Hospitality is an important element of the holistic approach to mentoring.

- Consider how you will create a welcoming, comfortable, loving, and safe environment for mentees to share, grow, and be challenged.

3 Elements of Hospitality:

1. **Confidentially:** Provide a copy of your mentoring group affirmations to all mentees, and hold everyone accountable to honoring the affirmations.

2. **Food & Fellowship:**

- Food – Consider how you will nourish the physical as well as the spiritual bodies of those entrusted to your care. Remember that mentees will most likely be rushing from another location prior to attending the mentoring group gathering. Ease their burdens by ensuring they know food will be provided. This is a way to serve them. Remember Jesus' instruction to his disciples at feeding of the crowd (Luke 9:12-13).

- Fellowship – Consider how you will engage the mentees in intentional conversation. Ensure that your time together supports the pillars of the ministry.

  Transparency and authenticity starts with you. Developing relationships of trust within the groups is equally important. Questions and conversations must challenge mentees to look to God, and take an honest look at themselves when considering their relationships with other people.

  Remember, this formal gathering only takes place once per month. Be present and give your undivided attention during the 3-hour session and expect the same from them.

  All cell phone and electronic devices—unless this is their means of accessing the Bible— must be turned off and put away. Consider a few minutes of quietness before praying or beginning. This centers all mentees' attention on the purpose of your time together.

3. **Mentoring Group Gathering Location:**

Particularly for outreach or evangelistic purposes, the church is not the best location for mentoring gatherings. "Home meetings" can be a critical asset to a large church and also provides a level of intimacy and privacy that may not occur as quickly in a church facility. Having "home meetings" in different locations throughout your city can also be very convenient and strategically offer different scheduling opportunities for people who normally drive a significant distance to get to church. If you cannot for some reason host a group gathering in your home, please prayerfully consider asking another person to host your mentoring group in their home.

[1] Luke 6: 12-13.

[2] Phil 2: 4.

[3] Eph. 4: 11-16.

[4] Prov. 22:1, Col. 4:5-6, 2 Tim. 2:21-26, and Titus 2:7-8.

[5] Mentor leaders are encouraged to regularly humble themselves before the Lord in prayer and teach their mentees to do the same. Through mentoring relationships, we humbly submit ourselves to each other out of reverence for Christ (Eph. 5: 21). We cultivate a teachable spirit which is a posture of humility. We are both teachers and students who admit that we don't know it all. We listen well and learn from others. We admit our mistakes and ask for forgiveness, and are open to all the ways God may want to move among us. We do not accept the position of leadership so we can hoard it over or control others. Rather, we see leadership as a privilege to model the leadership of Christ who came to serve and not be served (Matt. 20: 25-28 and Mark 10: 42-45). Concerning spiritual maturity, Paul writes that ministry leaders must not be new converts to the Christian faith (1 Tim. 3: 6). Mentors need spiritual maturity (Heb. 5:11-14), and Paul's instruction to Timothy lets us know that spiritual maturity is not always determined by one's age. Spiritually mature leaders have an ongoing thirst to passionately pursue God through their surrender to the teaching and power of the Holy Spirit, and discipline themselves to grow in their spiritual lives.

[6] For the first year of mentoring, I recommend the careful reading and discussion of Mentor for Life, along with the six lessons provided in this resource for the entire ministry team. As the ministry grows, you can ask mentors on the leadership team to prayerfully consider recommending future mentors/ministry leaders from the mentees in their mentoring groups. This is how you mentor and multiply, and this is how mentors and leaders are groomed within the ministry. When you groom mentor leaders from within the ministry, you do not have to start the leadership training from scratch at the beginning of every mentoring season. Based on the needs of the newly identified mentors, you can have each potential new mentor read Mentor for Life, evaluate their leadership skills and experience, and then selectively discern how to focus your mentoring leadership training lessons in the subsequent years.

[7] Peter F. Drucker, Managing the Non-profit Organization: Principles and Practices (New York, NY: Harper, 1990), 164.

[8] Ibid.

[9] Ibid, 169.

[10] C.J. Mahaney, Humility: True Greatness (Colorado Springs, CO: Multnomah Books, 2005), 22.

[11] J. Robert Clinton, The Making of a Leaders: Recognizing the Lessons and Stages of Leadership Development (Colorado Springs, CO: Navpress, 1988), 81.

[12] Reference Ephesians 4:11-16.

[13] "Mentee" is the word used throughout this resource to refer to the person being mentored. Some resources also use "mentoree" to define this person.

[14] Merriam-Webster, Incorporated, Merriam-Webster's Collegiate Dictionary, Tenth Edition (Springfield, Massachusetts: Merriam-Webster, Incorporated, 1996), 726.

[15] Take note of the mentoring relationships between Moses and Joshua, Naomi and Ruth, Elijah and Elisha, Mordecai and Esther, and Paul with Timothy or Titus.

[16] John 12:40, Acts 2:37, Acts 16:14, Acts 15:8-9, 2 Thess. 3:5, 2 Cor. 1:21-22, 2 Cor. 3:2-3, Eph. 3:17, Rom. 8:26-27, Rom. 2:29, and Heb. 8:10.

[17] Rick D Moore, "The prophet as mentor: a crucial facet of the biblical presentations of Moses, Elijah, and Isaiah," Journal of Pentecostal Theology 15, no. 2 (April 1, 2007): 155-172, ATLA Religion Database with ATLASerials, EBSCOhost (accessed July 9, 2012).

[18] Gal. 6:9-10, Eph. 2:10, James 2:14-26, Acts 2:42-47 and 4:32-37.

[19] John D. Lottes, "Jesus as mentor: biblical reflections for ministry with young adults," Currents in Theology and Mission 32, no. 2 (April 1, 2005): 128-138, ATLA Religion Database with ATLASerials, EBSCOhost (accessed July 9, 2012).

[20] A.W. Tozer, The Knowledge of the Holy (New York: HarperCollins, 1961), 1.

[21] Robert J. Wicks, Sharing Wisdom: The Practical Art of Giving and Receiving Mentoring (New York: The Crossroad Publishing Company, 2000), 115.

[22] 1 Cor. 12:7-31, Eph. 2:10 and Eph. 4:14-16.

[23] Darlene Zschech, The Art of Mentoring: Embracing the Great Generational Transition (Minneapolis, MN: Bethany House Publishers, 2011), 12.

[24] Luke 9:57-62 and Luke 14:25-35.

[25] Richard J. Foster, Celebration of Discipline: The Path to Spiritual Growth (New York, NY: HarperOne, 1998), 63.

[26] Jeffrey H. Mahan, Barbara B. Troxell, and Carol J. Allen, Shared Wisdom: A Guide to Case Study Reflection in Ministry (Nashville, TN: Abingdon Press, 1993), 117.

[27] Grenz, J. Stanley, David Guretzki & Cherith Fee Nordling. Pocket Dictionary of Theological Terms. Downers Grove, Il: IVP, 1999, 7.

[28] Ibid, 69.

[29] Ibid, 105.

[30] Grenz, J. Stanley, David Guretzki & Cherith Fee Nordling. Pocket Dictionary of Theological Terms. Downers Grove, Il: IVP, 1999, 55.

[31] Significant "Generations" research provided by Larry Diana, franchise owner of the Greensboro, NC Express Employment Professional's Office. Modified for this purpose and used with permission.

[32] Instructions for completion and a sample "Book Net-Out" are included in the appendices of this resource.

[33] The monthly discussion should assist the mentees in developing their book net-outs. Note: Book net-outs are not shared every month. They are only shared once the mentoring resource has been completed in its entirety.

[34] This is with exception of the first group gathering where each mentoring group member will share two prayer requests (one for that particular month and one long-term prayer request for the entire mentoring season).

[35] Note: I recommend a few mentoring resources at the end of Mentor for Life.

[36] Instructions for completion and a sample "Book Net-Out" are included in the appendices of this resource.

[37] Instructions for completion and a sample "Book Net-Out" are included in the appendices of this resource.

Made in the USA
Lexington, KY
30 August 2017